I0461373

The Story We Share

Jessi Bixler

Next Thing Press

Copyright © 2025 Jessi Bixler

All rights reserved. No part of this book may be reproduced, stored in a retrieval system, or transmitted in any form or by any means—electronic, mechanical, photocopying, recording, or otherwise be copied for public or private use—without the prior written permission of the author, except for brief quotations used in reviews, articles, or other critical works.

This is a work of nonfiction. The events described occurred as reported. Dialogues reflect the substance of conversations as remembered by the author and the individuals quoted, and where available, as supported by notes and court records. Some individuals are identified by role rather than full name to respect personal privacy. Any errors are the author's alone.

Cataloging-in-Publilcation Data is on file at the Library of Congress
Paperback: 979-8-9998653-0-4
Hardcover: 979-8-9998653-1-1
eBook: 979-8-9998653-2-8

For permissions, contact:
Next Thing Press
PO Box 6644, Lee's Summit, MO 64064
www.thestoryweshare.com
www.jessibixler.com

Cover design by: Miblart
Author photo by: Anne with a Cam

Printed in the United States of America

For Chad, who stood in the wreckage with me, steady, faithful, and never looking away.

And for my kids, who give me more reasons to heal than I can count. You both are the bravest parts of my story.

CONTENTS

A NOTE TO THE READER

If you're holding this book, I want to start by saying something simple but true: thank you.

I don't know exactly what brought you to these pages. Maybe you've lived through something that cracked your world open. Maybe someone you love has. Maybe you're here to better understand, to support, to heal, or to witness what too often goes unseen.

Whatever led you here, I want to acknowledge it with honesty and a little warning. This isn't an easy story. It is filled with pain and injustice, with the ache of silence and the failure of systems that were supposed to protect. It is about what happens after trauma and the long, uneven road toward healing.

And still, it is also a story of hope. Of growth. Of stubborn faith. It is about what it means to keep going when you are exhausted and angry and unsure of how any of this will ever make sense.

For me, a phrase became a lifeline: just do the next thing. When healing felt too big, I learned to take the next step. When justice failed, I shifted directions. When I didn't know how to keep going, I just kept showing up

I had been sharing my story in small settings for years, and often considered the idea of a book. But I waited, because the timing wasn't right. Then in the fall of 2024, I was talking with my therapist, who was undergoing cancer treatment. She told me she was writing a book. That simple moment, one woman quietly doing her next thing, nudged something in me. No flashing sign from God, no lightning bolt, but it was enough. Enough to begin. Enough to trust that maybe this was the time to tell my story.

You'll hear my voice throughout these chapters, but also the voices of those closest to me—my husband, my family, friends, even people within the legal system. Some of these people had a lot to say. Others had little – not because they didn't care or weren't affected but because they care so much and felt so deeply. We must all be careful not to compare one person's healing process to another's. The journey is long for everyone, but it is not the same. Because trauma does not just affect one person. And neither does healing.

You will not find perfect closure in these pages, but you will find truth. You will find anger, tenderness, questions, and grit. You will see what it costs to keep standing. You will see the strength it takes for a spouse to carry the weight of their partner's pain. And you will see what it looks like to rebuild a life, not all at once but one piece at a time.

A gentle note before you begin: some chapters contain references to sexual violence and descriptions of trauma and emotional pain that may be difficult to read. Take this book at your own pace. That may mean slowing down, skipping ahead, or setting it down when you need to. You are in charge.

What I hope you take away is this: healing is possible, even when it does not look the way you thought it would. And if all you can do today is just the next thing, that is enough.

THE BIRTHDAY PARTY

- 2013 -

"

I wanted everything that day to be perfect.

Jessi

Jessi

It was a typical November day for Kansas City. The wind was gusty. The temperature was cool but not freezing – although I thought it was plenty cold enough and was not looking forward to a Midwest winter. But on this day, we had no rain or snow. It was just a typical Saturday after Thanksgiving in KC.

At our house, though, things were anything but typical. Today was our daughter's first birthday, and I was ready. I had spent weeks (actually probably months) planning for this day. I spent hours on Pinterest looking for the perfect one-year-old birthday theme. It was her first birthday and one of our first opportunities to host a big family event in our new home, the one my husband Chad and I had been dreaming of for the past seven years. I wanted everything to be perfect.

When I got up that morning, a million details ran through my head. Had I picked up everything we needed for the party? Would our daughter tolerate her Alice in Wonderland tutu-style dress long enough for me to get some good pictures? Would the kids have fun?

After a week that included the hustle and bustle of a family Thanksgiving spent with my in-laws followed by Black Friday shopping, I wasn't sure who all would be able to make it to the party around their own holiday commitments, but that did not stop me from putting my heart and soul into it. I had gone all-in on the Alice in ONE-derland theme, spending weeks happily making lists, shopping, and getting everything ready. I was definitely more excited than my still shy-of-people daughter. It may seem silly that I had expended so much time and energy on a one-year-old's party. After all, she wouldn't remember it. But she was our only daughter, and I wanted the party to be something for me to remember, a special moment celebrating her and our brand new, beautiful home that we could share with our friends and family.

I had decided to lean into the vintage side of the Alice in Wonderland theme with invitations, appetizers, signs for each food, and party favors that included a bag of tea with an Alice in Wonderland-themed design. As a full-time working mom, I had done most of the planning in the evenings and on weekends, making multiple stops on my 45-minute commute home in the weeks leading up to the party. Now, all I had to do was take care of the finishing touches that would turn our home into a Wonderland of its own.

My mom and dad, Debbie and Tony, had come down from Omaha the night before and were staying with us even though my dad was struggling with the flu. No one wanted to miss my daughter's first birthday. In addition, Chad's parents and some of his family would be attending the party, including his cousin, her husband, and their son, who was the same age as our son. As I moved through the house putting up decorations and fixing food, I remember thinking that all I wanted was for this day to be perfect. Looking back on it, I think I made such an effort for this party because I wanted to celebrate that special connection between a mom and her first daughter and all the firsts we had experienced and those that were yet to come. I had even gone so far as to make my daughter an Alice in Wonderland blue tulle tutu, with a black headband and black Mary Jane shoes. I wanted to know when I looked at the pictures in the years to come that we had had this one perfect moment to celebrate her first year of life.

When the time for the party arrived, I looked around and smiled, giddy with excitement for this day and the memories we would make. The guests arrived, and the party began. It was everything I hoped it would be. I remember the warm feeling of seeing our family in our new home and the utter joy of thinking this would be the first of many times we would entertain like this, the first of the memories we would make. Chad and I had spent so much time deliberating over every detail of our new home, the one we planned to raise our kids in and grow old together in. Sharing it with our friends and family with our first real get-together to celebrate our daughter made it seem all our dreams had come to life.

Although the party was for my daughter, we didn't want our son to feel left out, so we let him and Chad's cousin's son help our daughter open her presents, as like most one-year-olds she was much more interested in the wrapping paper than she was in the actual gifts. We were hoping our son would get to know his second-cousin a bit better since they only lived a couple of hours away.

As the party wound down and we put a very tired one-year-old to bed, everyone was still having a good time, so we popped a couple of Costco pizzas in the oven, and the adults grabbed a beverage. In the way that family gatherings often do, the men congregated on the back porch, and the women sat at the kitchen table. I sipped my drink as I talked with my mom, enjoying how our relationship had changed since I had become a mom and could relate to her experiences in a different way now that I had children of my own. With the party decorations around us, I thought, "This has been a perfect day."

Little did I know, it was about to turn into a nightmare.

Jessi

Chad's cousin, her husband, and their son weren't people that would have normally come into town just for our child's birthday party. While Chad and his cousin had seen each other frequently growing up, we hadn't spent much time with them as couples. We had invited them to the party with the rest of Chad's family with the thought that it would be a great chance for our son to get to know their son since they were so close in age. We were also trying to make a conscious effort to spend more time with family. Like so many couples once they have kids, we had realized once more the importance of having those family connections in our lives.

As the evening wound down, we invited Chad's cousin and her family to spend the night with us, so they didn't have to make the two-hour drive home in the dark. They gladly accepted, and we set them up in the basement bedroom then went back upstairs to enjoy the pizza and some beers. Everyone who wasn't staying with us had left, and my mom eventually went to bed. Chad and the others were out on the lanai around the fireplace watching a sporting event of some sort. I was finishing the clean-up and would pop in and out of the conversation outside.

I had only met Chad's cousin and her husband a few times before this, and the husband had always rubbed me the wrong way. However, they were family, and even in my family there are people that I get along with better than others. The day of the birthday party was the most time we had ever spent with them as a couple. The conversation outside roamed from the game to the holidays and somehow the conversation turned to Chad's and my relationship.

Chad's cousin's husband (who I'm going to refer to as X from here on out because this is my story, and I don't want him to be at the center of it) started gushing about how great Chad and I were as a couple; he thought it was cool that we had met on eHarmony. It was slightly uncomfortable but mostly complimentary. Then the conversation turned. He brought up Chad's first marriage and started talking about how he wished he could get out of his own marriage; his wife was inside putting their son to bed. From my perspective, Chad's cousin was a nice woman. I had enjoyed talking with her throughout the day, and Chad had fond memories of her from his childhood. I started to get uneasy with the conversation.

Then X started disparaging his wife, calling her a "square," and I was reminded that he had previously made comments about how he thought it should be OK for men to beat their wives. I suddenly felt much less interested in getting to know Chad's cousin and her husband better.

At that point, my dad, who hadn't been feeling great, decided he was ready for bed and headed upstairs to join my mom. I was exhausted and took the opportunity to tell the others good night and headed back into the house. I finished up a few things in the kitchen and headed for our bedroom, which was on the main floor. I went through my normal nightly routine, washing my face and changing into my pajamas as I reflected on what a great day it had been, reliving the smiles and laughter and enjoying the warm feeling of having hosted those we love in our new home. I may have even pulled up a few photos on my phone before I set it aside for the night.

After a week of working, parenting, planning for Thanksgiving and the party, hosting, and cleaning up, I was exhausted. I fell into bed with a sigh, thankful for the memories but also thankful the event was over. Closing my eyes, I fell into a deep sleep almost immediately.

Chad

After Jess and Tony, her dad, went to bed, X and I sat out on the lanai for a few more minutes. I was tired but told my cousin's husband I'd stay up a bit longer and asked if he wanted another drink. Even though we had a keg in the basement, we had made a run to the liquor store earlier for Jameson Whiskey, his drink of choice. We decided we had both had enough alcohol, and he asked for a Gatorade or water. I told him we had Gatorade in the fridge inside, and he went inside to get one.

A few minutes passed, and he didn't come back out, so I assumed he had gone to bed. I started picking up outside, ready to head for bed myself. I put the fire out, swept the ashes off the patio and climbed a chair to put the cover back on the outdoor TV. As I was finishing up, Jess came running out — screaming.

Jessi

Like most couples, Chad and I had preferred sides of the bed. When I had gone to bed, I had laid down on my side with my back to Chad's empty place in the bed, knowing he would most likely be coming to bed shortly. I had fallen into a deep sleep almost immediately, exhaustion from the week catching up with me.

At some point, I felt hands reaching across me. Still mostly asleep, I assumed it was Chad snuggling in behind me. But my sleepy brain started to register something was wrong. The hands were rough — not at all like Chad's — and a voice was mumbling. I remember thinking it sounded cartoonish and breathy; the words were unrecognizable, but the voice itself had a physical weight that felt suffocating. Before I could comprehend what was happening, I felt him forcefully penetrate my vagina. Still not awake enough to fully understand what had happened, but knowing something was wrong, I rolled out of bed. I never looked behind me at the bed. I was shaken but actually thought I must have been dreaming.

I walked out of the bedroom in a daze and saw Chad on the lanai putting out the fire and covering up the TV. That's when I realized I hadn't been dreaming — and the person in my bed had not been my husband. I started screaming.

"It wasn't your hands! It wasn't your hands!"

Over and over again. That was all I could say.

Chad rushed in from outside, and I discovered I wasn't wearing pants or underwear. I had unconsciously been tugging on my pajama top to cover myself but had no idea that I was naked from the waist down. Chad wrapped his arms around me, trying to figure out what had happened, and my parents came running from their upstairs bedroom at the sound of my screams, and Chad's cousin had arrived from the basement.

At that moment, X came out of our bedroom. Chad had begun to understand what had happened, and he got between me and X. Despite still not understanding what had happened, Chad's cousin and my mom helped to usher X to the basement, away from me.

I don't remember a lot of what happened next. I do remember retreating to our bathroom, curling up on the floor and sobbing. At some point, the decision was made to call the police. Before they got to the house, I decided I had to get the sheets off our bed. I couldn't stand to look at them and furiously removed them with Chad's help. While we were stripping them from the bed, I found my pants and underwear and put them back on. We put the sheets in a pile by the stairs going up to the laundry room. I don't know why I thought I would ever wash those sheets and use them again.

Later, I came out of the bathroom and saw X being led away in handcuffs. His wife was crying and asking why we were doing this. I remember apologizing to her, as if this were somehow my fault.

One of the officers stayed at our house while the other took X to the police station. I don't remember what the police officer said until he told me I needed to go to the hospital to be examined.

Chad

When I heard Jess screaming, I was still up on the chair covering up the TV, and I didn't know what was wrong. I thought maybe she had had a nightmare or something had happened inside the house. My first concern was simply calming her down and figuring out what had upset her. I gave her a half-hug, and that's when I realized she wasn't wearing pants.

She kept saying, "They weren't your hands! They weren't your hands!" I was beginning to put the pieces together when we walked back inside. That's when I saw X coming out of our bedroom, adjusting his shirt. He was trying to talk to Jess, and I think he was saying he was sorry. I didn't care. I just knew I had to get him away from Jess. I put myself between them and stiff-armed him to keep him away.

The sound of Jess's screams had woken her parents, and they came down the stairs. My cousin had come up from the basement. X kept repeating, "I'm sorry."

People asked me later how I managed not to hit him, but I was in shock and only focused on keeping Jess safe. The reality of what had happened didn't set in until later. At that moment, I just wanted him to go downstairs to get as far away from Jess as possible.

While I dealt with my cousin and X, Jess's mom took Jess into our bathroom, where Jess collapsed on the floor. Her mom came out a little bit later and said, "We need to call the cops." I hadn't even thought about calling the cops, and at first, I was unsure about it. I'm not sure why that was. I think we were all still in shock. After talking it over with Jess's parents, we all agreed to call the police.

I went and sat on the bathroom floor with Jess while her parents called the police without telling my cousin and X. She had basically just collapsed onto the floor in a tight fetal position, crying hysterically. I don't know how much time passed, but it was mostly just me holding her on the floor while she cried.

The officers arrived and asked us some questions. That initial conversation with the police is a blur, but I know they talked to me, Jess's mom, and Jess before going downstairs to arrest X.

X and his wife were downstairs and had not heard the police come in. When the officers brought X upstairs, he was the one that was angry.

"What are you doing?" he yelled at me.

His wife followed up saying, "Don't do this to our family."

X's actions had irrevocably changed my family. How ironic that he and his wife were blaming us for that harm.

Mom/Debbie

I woke up to Jess's screams. No matter how old your kids are, the sound of them screaming will immediately spur you into action. I shot out of bed and ran downstairs. When I got downstairs, I saw Chad arguing with X and could hear Jess sobbing somewhere in the background. I didn't know what had happened, but I knew Chad was trying to get X far away from Jess. I thought maybe X had said something awful that had upset Jess. I told Chad to let me handle X and to go be with Jess. Still not knowing what was wrong with my daughter, I argued with X. I told X's wife she needed to take him downstairs, but X elbowed her out of the way. X's wife looked at me and said, "I don't know what to do when he's drinking." After a few more minutes, we finally convinced him to go downstairs.

With that task taken care of, I went to check on my daughter. I found her curled up in a fetal position in her bedroom closet, and I knew whatever had happened was much worse than I had imagined.

"What happened?"

"He raped me."

I was in shock. I didn't know what to do, but then I thought, "We need to call the police."

Chad and I discussed it a little bit before he agreed. Jess seemed OK with whatever we wanted to do.

I ran upstairs and told my then-husband what had happened, and we called the police.

The whole time I kept thinking, "How is this possible? How could this happen?" We were in Jess's home. How could she not have been safe? I couldn't even grasp the possibility. I kept thinking it was a nightmare, and I would wake up. Over and over again, I said to myself, "This can't be real. This isn't happening to us."

The police arrived. They took the bedding from Jess and Chad's bed and told X's wife that he would need a lawyer. I didn't know what to do. I felt helpless. I sat and waited while the police talked to everyone and told Jess she needed to go to the hospital. As the police officer was getting ready to leave, X's wife asked Chad if he wanted to press charges. That's when the dam broke, and the anger came flooding out. Before Chad could answer, I screamed, "Yes, he raped her. We're going to press charges."

Looking back, I know I shouldn't have spoken for Chad, but at the time I was — and still am — so angry that this happened to my daughter.

Dad/Tony

I had gone to bed not long after my then-wife and Jess had gone to bed. I woke up to Jess screaming, so I got dressed and ran down the stairs to see what was wrong. I had the flu, so I wasn't in great shape. When I got downstairs, Debbie, Chad and X were standing at the foot of the stairs. I'm trying to figure out what is going on, and all I know is that Debbie and Chad are trying to get X to go downstairs. His wife comes up, and we finally get him to go downstairs. He just kept saying he was sorry, but I had no clue what he was sorry for. Debbie went in to check on Jess, and I went back upstairs because I didn't know what had happened and I didn't know what else to do.

A little bit later, Debbie comes back upstairs and tells me we need to call the police because Jess had been raped. When I found out, the only thing I felt was an indescribable anger and helplessness. I went back downstairs and waited for the police while Debbie went in to be with Chad and Jess. I let the police in, and they went down and got X and took him out of Jess and Chad's home.

Police

Deputies Barton and Darks arrived at the house in response to Debbie Mell's call. They met Debbie in the driveway, and she escorted them into the house where they spoke to Chad then Jessi.

In the police report, Deputy Barton said:

> "I then made contact with Mrs. Bixler (victim) who was wearing a white-in-color shirt with brown pants. Based on my initial observations of Mrs. Bixler it was apparent that she was visibly upset and had been crying. Mrs. Bixler's eye make up was still running down both her left and right cheek, and her eyes were red and bloodshot."

After speaking with Jessi and Chad, Deputy Barton reported that:

> "Darks and I then went to the downstairs portion of the home where a guest room had been set up. I knocked on the door and identified myself as a Sheriff's Deputy and placed (suspect) in mechanical hand restraints and placed him in the rear of Darks' patrol vehicle. The suspect was

standing in the guest bedroom talking with his wife. The suspect was visibly intoxicated with watery, bloodshot eyes, and slurred speech."

Deputy Darks' report reads:

"Deputy Barton and I proceeded downstairs where the suspect was located and took him into custody at that time, and he was secured in the rear of my patrol vehicle. While in my vehicle (without being asked any questions) the suspect stated that 'I only remember being in bed with my wife, now I'm in the back of a police car.'"

At this point, the deputies decided to call in a detective. Deputy Barton wrote in his report:

"I then contacted Detective Henderson who advised that he would be enroute to meet myself and Mrs. Bixler at Centerpoint hospital to conduct an informal interview. Detective Henderson stated to me that he would contact Detective Edwards who would respond to the scene for photographs and processing of the crime scene. I then told Mrs. Bixler that she would need to go to Centerpoint so that a Rape Kit could be completed. Mrs. Bixler stated that she would like a family member to go with her to the hospital and did not want to ride in my patrol car. Mrs. Bixler's father drove his vehicle and followed me to Centerpoint hospital."

Detective Edwards arrived at the home and reported that:

"I contacted the suspect who was being held in a patrol vehicle in the driveway of the residence, [He] stated that he had been instructed by his father not to make any statements without having an attorney present. At that time I instructed Deputy Darks to transport the suspect to the Jackson County Detention Center and book him on a 24 hour investigative hold in regard to a rape."

Deputy Darks transported the suspect to the police station where the police report states he "was given a portable breath test as part of admissions procedures, and his reading was .092."

THE HOSPITAL

"

Sometimes when patients come in, they've just been violated, they feel very exposed. And so they will frequently try to close in, kind of like mummy or papoose, like you do a small child, to feel secure and comfortable.

Susan Kiger, RN.

Jessi

I know the police came and took X away. My mom and Chad had made the decision to call the police because I wasn't able to make decisions. I just went along with what they thought was best. The police said I needed to go to the hospital to be examined, and at some point it was decided that my dad would take me to the hospital because I didn't want to ride in the police car. I got in the car and lay my head on the door and pulled my knees into a ball and began sobbing and shaking. I kept repeating, "It wasn't his hands, it wasn't Chad's hands." My dad didn't say a word. He tried to comfort me, but I could hear his sobs through my own. He was struggling to breathe and shaking so bad I could feel it when he tried to pat my back to get me to calm down. I simply leaned against the window and did what many sexual assault victims do: I dissociated.

Dissociation is a common response to trauma where a survivor will detach from reality. It is a defense mechanism that allows the brain to cope with the trauma of sexual assault, and those who experience dissociation often say they feel as if they are watching what is happening from outside their body. That's what it felt like for me, as if I was watching myself riding in the car with my dad from above the situation.

I entered the hospital, and it seemed like the whole world was moving in slow motion, as if my brain simply needed more time to process everything that was happening. I remember looking at the people in the waiting room, thinking, "I'm not one of you" followed immediately by the opposite thought, "I am one of you." I didn't want any of this to be real, and each step into the hospital meant that this assault had really happened.

As soon as the hospital personnel understood what had taken place, they immediately took me and my dad back to the exam room to wait for the sexual assault nurse examiner to arrive. My dad stayed until the nurse came in. Then, as it does for so many sexual assault survivors, the nightmare got even worse. The exam was horrible, and it took hours. They swabbed me everywhere, took pictures, asked personal questions, and watched me pee. After already having been violated through sexual assault, the exam prolonged the trauma. It was invasive and traumatizing.

Sexual assault exams, often called rape kits, are a crucial piece of evidence gathering after a sexual assault, but gathering that evidence requires invading the space and privacy of an already traumatized victim. Often those victims are like me, alone and in a dissociative state, and even though sexual assault nurse examiners are specially trained to work with sexual assault victims, nothing makes this humiliating process easier for the victim.

An advocate from the Metropolitan Organization Countering Sexual Assault (MOCSA) arrived, but I didn't want to talk to her. MOCSA would become important to my story later, but right now, it felt like talking to them was another step in accepting what had happened to me that I was not ready for. The MOCSA advocate left behind a bag with clothes and brochures because the nurse examiner had taken my clothes as evidence. Losing my clothes was one of the most upsetting things because I was wearing a shirt I had gotten in college. One of my close friends in college was a talented artist who died of an epileptic seizure. I had advocated for those shirts to be made after he died that featured his artwork. Besides some photographs, it was the only thing I had left of him. To make matters worse, the clothes they had given me in the bag were awful – a Hanes T-shirt, blue sweatpants, and granny panties – things I would never choose to wear but were now my only option.

The nurse handed me some pills – a morning after pill and some antibiotics – then I gave a formal statement to the police, and my dad took me home, but I didn't remember the drive. Chad's cousin and her son were already gone when I arrived. I hugged Chad, took the pills, and threw away the awful clothes from the hospital and all the brochures from MOCSA.

Police

After leaving the Bixlers' home, Detective Edwards met Jessi at the hospital for an informal interview. He recounts the brief interview in his police report:

"Upon arrival at Centerpoint I contacted the victim who was being treated for the rape. I advised the victim that I would be obtaining a brief statement from her at this time and would like to contact her at a later time the next day to do a formal interview. The victim gave me a brief accounting of what had transpired, basically the same information as I had obtained from her husband, and stated that she would like some time to think about what had happened before she made any more statements, or any decisions on prosecution."

Susan Kiger, RN.

Susan Kiger was the forensic nurse examiner that did the rape kit on Jessi. She described the process and her thoughts during later court testimony. This narrative is drawn from that testimony.

Kiger was at home when the call came in to her pager at 1:43 a.m. that a forensic nurse examiner was needed at Centerpoint Medical Center. When she called the hospital she was told a female sexual assault had occurred around 11 p.m. on Nov. 30.

After taking the call, Kiger activated the Metropolitan Organization Countering Sexual Assault (MOCSA). In her court testimony, she described MOCSA like this:

> "They send out advocates that are trained in...handling and helping individuals of sexual assault with the exam process. Sometimes our young ladies appear–they don't have any family or friends to be with them, and so they are there to offer support during the exam. Then they also explain to them services that are available through MOCSA for them after the exam."

Kiger arrived at Centerpoint at 2:24 a.m., where after checking in with security to get the keys to the forensic exam room, she met up with Jessi. Kiger described meeting Jessi in her testimony:

"I proceeded to the emergency room where I met with Ms. Bixler. I explained the exam process to her. She was accompanied by her father. She gave me both verbal and written consent at that time. And then I believe she was in emergency room 26. And so we left the emergency room proper and went to the forensic exam room. Her father came with us. He sat in the room adjoining our exam room. And then at that point the exam would have began."

The consent forms were extensive, including consent to test for pregnancy, sexually transmitted diseases, to do an examination, and to take photographs. Before the physical examination began, Kiger asked Jessi to tell her what had happened, which helped Kiger determine at which points on the victim's body she might find evidence. The exam also includes a physical inspection for injuries. Kiger described the process in court:

"In a lot of instances the patient does not have any trauma that they feel needs to be seen by a physician. But when the patient is then released to me, I have an obligation when I'm doing my assessment to make a determination that they either do or do not have injuries that may warrant my needing to take them back to the emergency department. So even though you might say an assault occurred below the waist, I still start my evaluation from the top down and I examine them. I'm looking for bruises, abrasions, lacerations, anything that might be a physical trauma."

Kiger also makes an assessment of a rape victim's emotional state and takes note of their demeanor. She described Jessi like this:

"She was crying, and at times throughout the exam you could tell she was trying to fight back crying. She was upset that the incident occurred. She was in disbelief that it happened, I guess, because this was a family member. She sat I say, you know, closed in. Her arms around her. She had on a jacket, and she kept kind of twisting and closing it in. Sometimes when patients come in, they've just been violated, they feel very exposed. And so they will frequently try to close in, kind of like mummy or papoose, like you do a small child, to feel secure and comfortable. And she was exhibiting that, you know. I don't know how to describe it all. I mean, she sits very stiff backed and straight up in the chair, like I say, closing her arms in, twisting on her jacket, trying to feel kind of small and secure."

Kiger finished her exam and made a final assessment:

"She was a neat, clean, well nourished female. When I laid eyes on, so to speak, initially, I didn't see any outward physical signs of bruising or any kind of trauma in that aspect. I did not find any holes or tears, anything in the clothing to indicate that maybe clothes had been torn or ripped off of her, anything like that. So again, nothing outwardly to show visible physical trauma. Again, the question regarding a lapse or decrease in consciousness, I had marked yes just for a decrease in consciousness because she was asleep at the time."

Dad/Tony

We decided I would take Jess to the hospital. I think the police needed to talk to Chad, and as her dad, I didn't want to let her out of my sight. I had already not been able to protect her from the assault. I think I needed to know she was safe, so we followed the police officer to the hospital. The drive was awful. Jess was totally destroyed. She just cried and cried, and I couldn't do anything to help.

When they took her in the room by herself, I just sat and tried to wrap my head around what had happened. I didn't know what to do. There were so many people going in and out. I know MOCSA came. I just remember feeling concerned about Jess and so helpless. There wasn't much that I could do.

On the way home, she curled up on the seat again and cried and cried.

Chad

While Jess was gone, X's dad came to pick up my cousin and her son. I helped her carry her son out of our son's room where they were both still sleeping, downstairs and get their stuff out of the house. Now, it seems odd to me that X's dad came to get them. Their white pickup with a dirt bike in the back was parked in our garage. My cousin continued to ask me not to tell the family, "it's going to ruin the family, though." I told her I loved her, but what X did was wrong. She responded by saying, "I'm never going to tell my parents about this, so please don't tell your mom." I found that statement confusing. I was still trying to wrap my head around what had happened, and I couldn't see any way that my parents would not find out about it. And I had to wonder had he done something like this before that I wasn't aware of? I was shocked that she would ask me not to tell my mom, but I also felt some sympathy for my cousin that her first response was to cover up what had happened and bury it, which never leads to anything good.

After she left, Jess's mom and I stayed awake, sitting in the living room waiting for Jess and her dad to get back. When Jess came in, it was early morning, and she was closed off from all of us, still crying, and not talking to anyone. She went into our bedroom and curled up in a fetal position. Sometimes she would cry hysterically and other times she would just lay there with a blank stare, like there was no one inside her head.

I was still in shock, too, at first just trying to figure what had happened then trying to figure out how to best protect everyone and make sure they were all OK. The emotions of it all were just starting to come to the surface. Definitely pain and anger and a lot of second-guessing about things I could have done to prevent it from happening. And even though I'm usually a very calm person there was anger. A lot of anger.

FILING A POLICE REPORT

"

Do you think he intended to do what he did?

Jackson County Detective

Jessi

I slept most of the day on Sunday, but Monday morning came and even though everything had changed for me, the world outside kept moving along as if everything was the same. I've always been a doer, so in the aftermath of the assault, I focused on just doing the next thing. On Monday morning, the next thing was going to the police station to give a formal statement. I had spoken to the police on Saturday night and early Sunday morning, both at my house and at the hospital, but that had been brief, just enough information that they would be able to hold X for 24 hours. On this day, I would have to give them all the details that my mind was working so hard to block out.

Both Chad and my parents went to the police station with us along with our brother-in-law Michael, who is a lawyer. The police took my statement and Chad's statement separately. I walked alone into an interview witness room with a female detective. However, the recording equipment wasn't working in that room, so we ended up in a small interrogation room like the ones you see on TV in shows like "Law & Order", complete with a ring for handcuffs on the table. I was traumatized and uncomfortable as I recounted the details of the assault. At one point, the detective turned off the recording, shut her notebook and laid down her pen.

"Do you think he intended to do what he did?" she asked.

I didn't know how to answer. I hadn't done anything wrong, but all I could think of was all the police shows I had seen on TV where the police try to trick people into saying something incriminating. I know that made little sense. I was the victim, but I was traumatized and alone, so I gave a noncommittal answer because I was scared to say the wrong thing. I didn't really know X all that well even though he was part of my extended family. I truly didn't know what he was thinking, but in my mind I was screaming, "How could he not intend to do what he did?"

But what came out of my mouth was, "I couldn't speculate."

"I want you to speculate," she said.

I tried again to avoid the question. "I can't remember."

She repeated her original question. "Do you think he intended to do or meant to do what he did?"

I still felt cautious, but I was exhausted and wanted this to be over. "Yes," I said. And that was the truth.

"Good," she said. "I do, too. Let's take a break."

She took me out the back door of the police station and offered me a cigarette, which I declined. As she lit her own cigarette and we stood out there, I wondered again if this was still part of the interview. Was she trying to get me to say something else? What were we doing out here? My brain simply could not think rationally, and I think it was telling that even at the police station, I didn't feel safe and had a level of paranoia about the process that in a more rational state of mind I might not have had.

The detective shared with me that she, too, had been a victim of a traumatic event. Looking back, I can see that she was trying to make me feel less alone, but at the time, I simply could not process someone else's trauma. I just wanted to wind the clock back to my daughter's birthday party and have none of this ever happen.

After we went back inside, the detective gave me a list of next steps.

"Here's what you need to do next: first thing, you need to get a restraining order, but then you need to go see your primary care doctor and then you need to go talk to someone," she said.

Finally, here was something my brain *could* process. I had a list. I had things to do. I didn't have to think. I didn't have to plan. I could just do the next thing on my list.

But before we could start on that list, Chad had to give his statement, and we had to tell my parents goodbye. They had stayed one more day than they had planned, but they both had jobs they needed to get back to in Omaha. At the time, I don't think it bothered me that they were leaving. I didn't have a huge capacity to think about how I was feeling and how other people's actions were affecting me, but looking back, I know that my parents' leaving so soon after the event contributed to making me feel like I had to re-enter the regular routine of my life – long before I was ready.

Chad

I gave my statement to the police that day. I sat down with the detectives, hoping they would put me at ease that they would build a case against X, but they seemed dismissive. I don't remember everything they said, but one thing does stand out: When I was in with the detectives, they sat me down and very seriously said to me something like, "I just want to let you know that your marriage is probably over because 80 percent of marriages where a woman is sexually assaulted end in divorce."

Whether that statistic was exact or not, it was shattering. Those words sent my body into fight mode, not in an aggressive or confrontational way, but more in a determination to prove them wrong. I don't remember what I said back to them, but I know I was thinking, "Just because you say that doesn't make it true. If you think I can't hold my family together, let me prove you wrong."

From that moment on, my whole goal was to give Jess whatever she needed, so that we would not be just another statistic. (Note: No actual statistics exist on the number of marriages that end in divorce after sexual assault, but we do know that 60% of marriages where one spouse suffers from PTSD, which is common among sexual assault survivors, end in divorce.)

In addition to coping with this new information, I was also still trying to manage my own emotions about what had happened. I had run through a gamut of emotions in the 48 hours since the event from confusion to feeling overprotective of both Jess and the kids to pain that this had happened to overwhelming anger. But the emotion that hit the hardest was the overwhelming sense of hopelessness. I had failed to protect my family, and I didn't know how to fix it. I didn't cry at the police station, but over the next few days, I would find a place to be alone and let those emotions bubble to the surface to be released in tears. I also spent a lot of time questioning everything: Why did we have them spend the night? What could I have done differently? Have I ruined my wife and kids forever? Even now, I still doubt myself, but in those first hours and days, those emotions were strong.

In addition, I knew that with Tony and Debbie leaving, we were going to have to start focusing on our 1- and 4-year old kids more and picking back up the threads of our day-to-day lives, something I wasn't sure Jess was ready for.

Mom/Debbie

We went with Jess and Chad to the police station on Monday, but there wasn't anything for us to do. They didn't need to talk to us. So, we went home. We had to go back to work. It was hard because I wanted to stay there with Jess, but I wasn't sure how to help. It's not something you learn or think you need to know. I thought, "I raised her to be independent. She has a family and a life of her own."

I didn't know what to do, and I didn't know how to help. But something told me, I need to remember all of this, so I went home and wrote it all down. I thought, "I'm going to need to know this and share this at some point. And for however many years it was, I replayed it in my head because I wanted to be able to tell the story. In my mind, that was how I was going to help.

I also remember being so angry. It was the worst day of my life. I was really angry at her dad. I kept thinking, "Why didn't you do something?" In my mind, I expected him to go beat the shit out of this guy, but he hadn't done anything. I was just really mad.

Dad/Tony

We stayed another day. I called in for work because there was no way we were going back until we knew everything was good. I don't even know if it was Monday or Tuesday that we came back. We would have liked to stay. Unfortunately, it was just really hard to leave her and not know how she was going to be. It's probably one of the hardest things that I ever had to do. I didn't know how she was doing? What could we do to help? Unfortunately, you have to go on and go back to work. It's what we all have to do, but it was just terrible.

Jessi

After we left the police station, I insisted that we stop to get new sheets for the bed. I stood in the bedding aisle staring at the dozens of options for sheets, thinking "I don't want to spend $100 on new sheets. Mine are perfectly fine." But they weren't fine. I remember thinking those sheets were tainted, soiled and trashed, just like me. With new sheets in hand, I was left with the question of what do I do next? How do I continue living the life I was living before the assault?

At the time, I was still in a daze, but looking back, that moment when my body was violated closed a book on the Jessi that had existed for the first 31 years of my life. After the rape, a new Jessi would take her place, one that resembled the old Jessi in some ways but who would, in other ways, be entirely different. Sexual assault doesn't just violate your body. It violates your soul. It changes everything: your sense of self, your marriage, your parenting, your relationships with family and friends, your sense of safety – even in your own home. In the months and years ahead, I would have to figure out who that new Jessi was and how she fit into the old Jessi's life, but in those first few days after the rape, I was just trying to put one foot in front of the other and do the things I thought needed to be done.

I went back to work on Tuesday. I really don't even know what I was thinking. I obviously needed time to process what had happened to me, but this was my life, and I needed to go back to it. I think I was in denial – thinking that if I just kept chugging along then maybe it wouldn't be real. All I could think about was what had happened to me, with memories of the last 72 hours floating through my head on a constant reel. Driving to work was the worst part, staring out at the scenery on the same route I had taken five days a week for over five years, everything seemed foreign. I constantly checked my mirrors, my heart leaping in fear any time I saw a white truck. It was like waiting for a bomb to drop.

When I had called my boss on Sunday to tell him what happened, he had told me to take all the time I needed, but I didn't know what else to do. Going back to work seemed like the next thing on the list.

I didn't speak to anyone for a month straight, simply answering questions with one-word responses. I didn't recognize my own voice. Whenever I had to walk anywhere – the bathroom, lunch, the car – I looked down at my feet because I didn't want to see what was coming. The few times that I passed a male co-worker in the hall, although not necessarily obvious to them, I would pull away. I remember thinking, "Now they know what happened, they can see right through you."

One of my friends and co-workers, John, finally asked if I was okay, and I started to cry. He asked me to come to his office where I told him what happened. Just as I had with the phone call to my aunts and uncles, I struggled to get the words out through the tears and the shaking. When I finally did, he said, "Holy shit, Jessi. I am so, so sorry. What the hell are you doing here? You shouldn't be here."

He was right. I shouldn't have been there. I was still in shock and struggling with all the things that rape survivors have to deal with. I was still in denial—and often dissociating. Working was hard. Parenting was hard. Talking was hard. Nothing was easy. The whole world looked different, as if I was looking through someone else's eyes. I simply went through the motions, sometimes watching myself from a dissociated distance, knowing that woman was me, but not wanting to live with the emotions and trauma she was experiencing.

We went to court to get a restraining order about two weeks later. The initial paperwork process was just another impersonal hoop to jump through. The Adult Abuse department was on the second floor of the Jackson County Courthouse in a dingy room with stained, 30-year-old carpet. It reminded me of the DMV with employees who showed the same enthusiasm for their jobs as those at the DMV. They handed over the paperwork and told us we could take it home or fill it out there. I didn't want to have to come back, but I couldn't stay in that office another minute, so we took it out into the hallway to fill it out. We filled out the three-page document and returned it to be filed. It was Dec. 3. On Dec. 10, X was served, and our court date was set for Dec. 17.

We hadn't heard from X or his wife since the assault, nor did we want to, but I knew X would be at the hearing. I was not prepared to see him again. When we arrived, I was a mess. Some women from Hope House, a local non-profit that helps women in domestic abuse situations, saw that I was visibly upset and asked what was wrong.

"I was raped, and he's here," I said.

Immediately, the women stepped in to help.

"Oh my goodness," one of them said. "Let's go around the hall."

Those women were so wonderful. They sat me down and surrounded me, so I would not need to see X. Then they sent someone into the courtroom to identify which side of the courtroom he was on and to wait until my case was called, so I could sit in the hallway instead of in the courtroom where I would need to be near X. I waited with them until my case was called.

Some people might think stepping into a courtroom to face your attacker is a liberating experience, but for me, it was not. I was two weeks away from the assault, and my attacker was standing just a few feet from me as we approached the judge.

Retraumatization is a word used to describe what happens to sexual assault victims every time they have to tell their story, especially in the criminal justice system. The American criminal justice system is not kind to victims of sexual assault. We are made to retell our stories over and over again. We can be questioned about anything from what we were wearing to how many drinks we had, always with the inference that maybe we had done something wrong, something to invite the attack. It is a cruel way to find justice, and many sexual assault survivors never do.

While a restraining order hearing is fairly simple and quick, it does require the underlying facts for the order to be laid out. Standing there, knowing the judge was judging the truthfulness and credibility of my statement only added to my trauma. Thankfully, the proceedings were quick, and I left the courtroom with my restraining order in hand and a slight sense of comfort that if X approached me again, he could be arrested. I thought this would be the first of many court victories in criminal court. I didn't know it would be my only one.

Chad

Those first few weeks after the rape were brutal. Jess tried to go back to work, and I really hoped it would provide a change of environment and help her to heal. However, I was worried that it was too soon, but she wanted to go back and I wanted her to have the freedom to make that choice. I also had to work, but now I also needed to be both mom and dad to our young kids. Jess had no capacity to be a constant parent. While she did engage with the kids when she could, I became the go-to parent when the kids needed comfort, discipline, playtime, questions answered, or someone to help them. When she was home, Jess was often not mentally present. Our entire dynamic was off. When someone goes through that kind of trauma, it just takes time for them to come back. I was trying so hard to take care of everything the kids needed but also to still provide support for Jess to make sure she had what she needed to recover and heal.

I was definitely driven by the words that those police officers had said about my marriage being over. I love Jess. I didn't want this thing that happened that neither of us could control to be the thing that ended us. I was in it for the long haul. Whatever she needed, I wanted her to have it. I just wanted her to come back to us. It would be a while before I realized that we would never get back the old Jess. She had been changed in ways that we couldn't undo. I knew that we would have to grow together to figure out how our family needed to change to graft the changes in Jess into our new dynamic.

When we went to court to get the restraining order, I was not allowed in the room. The courtroom itself was small and they were only allowing immediate people who had cases on the docket. I had to wait outside with X's dad. We didn't speak. We didn't look at each other. The waiting was awful. I just kept wondering if Jess was okay and if the hearing was going well while I was stuck in the waiting room with a man I couldn't stand to look at, trying to keep all my anger, rage, sadness, helplessness, and worry in check. I just wanted that day to be over.

TELLING FAMILY

"

Retraumatization doesn't just happen in the justice system. It can happen every time a sexual assault survivor is asked to re-tell their story.

Jessi

Jessi

Nothing is easy in the wake of a sexual assault. Just getting out of bed is hard. For me, the thought of telling someone what had happened seemed impossible. But knowing what to do after something like this happens is hard for everyone, even the people who love the sexual assault survivor. Sometimes, what seems like the right thing to do for your loved ones is exactly the wrong thing to do for the survivor.

Not long after the assault, my mom asked me to share what had happened with the rest of the family in a group call. I think she thought it would be easier for me to just tell my story once rather than have to tell it multiple times. But I wasn't ready to tell anyone. I was still coming to terms with my new reality. I didn't want to share that reality with anyone else – even people who loved me unconditionally.

I wasn't in any shape, however, to make a logical argument that I wasn't ready. I'm not sure I could have even articulated what I was feeling at the time about telling other people, so I agreed to do the call. I had asked my mom not to tell anyone, and I remember telling Chad I thought it would be good for her to have some support.

So, that evening I sat on the couch and my mom called my cell phone. She had only told the family that I had something that I wanted to tell everyone all at once. I can't imagine what they thought I had to say, but I know telling them I had been raped was definitely nowhere on their lists. When the phone rang, I started shaking. Chad sat next to me for support. I took a deep breath and asked if everyone was in the room. If I was going to do this, I was only doing it once.

I began to speak: "This weekend, on the night of Aria's birthday, we had family over including Chad's cousin and her husband. They decided to stay the night. He and Chad were having drinks on the lanai and I went to bed. When I woke up, I felt hands on my body and... he raped me."

I managed to get it out. I was shaking and sobbing, and I didn't feel any better. In fact, I felt worse.

A female voice on the other line said "What!"

I'm not sure who it was. I'm not sure I cared.

I think they asked me some questions, mostly showing concern and asking if I was OK. I wasn't OK. I wasn't sure I would ever be OK again. At that point, I could hardly speak and I had done my part, so I asked them to talk to mom and dad if they had more questions. They told me they loved me, and we said goodbye.

Retraumatization doesn't just happen in the justice system. It can happen every time a sexual assault survivor is asked to re-tell their story, especially in the time before the survivor has had time to process and heal themselves. I know that my mom would never have intentionally caused me pain. She thought she was doing the right thing, trying to make it easier to tell people that she thought needed to know. The aftermath of a sexual assault is hard – for everyone.

Mom/Debbie

I asked Jess to share her story with the family because I thought it would be easier for her to only share it once, so everybody heard the same story at the same time and got the same information. I was worried the family would talk and the facts would get lost as the story got passed around. I didn't want Jess's story to be different from what it was.

The phone call was hard. It was really the first time we had said out loud what had happened outside of telling the police. I didn't know what to expect from my family. They all were very good. But I think like me, they didn't know what to do or how to react. We've never really talked much about it since. My one sister, Patti, and I have talked a little bit about it over the years and she has come to some of the advocate activities Jess has been involved in. Other than that, no one's ever talked about it since. It has never really come up.

I wanted to be able to tell someone, to tell my friends. I wanted to talk to someone about what I had experienced.

Aunt Loretta

I was on the family call when Jess told everyone what had happened. The call was very sad. It was. It hurt me deeply. The family had a lot of different comments about "How could this possibly happen?" I remember one of my brothers wanted to go out and buy Jess a new mattress immediately. There was just a lot of shock and hurt and not understanding how this could have occurred.

There was a lot of anger and there still is a lot of anger from Jess's mom (my sister) about the situation. I think that anger was a way for her to deal with the situation because this is her daughter.

My sister Patti and I decided we needed to go down and see Jess. We just felt that we needed to be there in any way that we could, whether it was just being there and not saying anything, just being there for the hug. On the ride down we just talked about how could something like this possibly happen to somebody that we love so very much.

Patti and I stayed together in the upstairs guest bedroom. Jess and Chad offered that one of us could stay in the basement guest bedroom, but Jess said she couldn't bring herself to go down there yet. At some point, I decided I was going to go down there and change the sheets on the bed. I removed them, washed them and put them back on the bed. I thought it was the least I could do and might be a small gesture to ease the burden she was feeling.

We spent the weekend, and the thing I remember most was going to a bowling event for Jess's work. I just watched and in my heart absorbed her emotions. Her daughter was there, and I just held her. Jess was in a different world at that time. She seemed scared and confused, like she didn't know where she was. She didn't say anything to any of the people she worked with. I remember hugging her several times, but she just seemed like she was in a different world.

I still don't like talking about it and to know that that happened to one of my babies. I didn't want to know the details. I didn't want to know any of that. I just wanted to be someone to hold her.

Aunt Patti

I found out about the rape when I was invited to a family meeting at one of my brother's house. We got there and nobody knew what it was about. When I got to the house, I saw my sister Debbie, Jess's mom, coming out of the bedroom with my sister-in-law, and she was visibly upset. I kept thinking, "Oh my God, what is going on?" Even then, I could not have imagined what I was going to hear.

We all gathered in the basement and called Jess. She was on speakerphone, and she told us what happened. I looked around the room, and Debbie was visibly upset. Her dad Tony was there, too, and he's usually a happy-go-lucky guy, but he was just sitting there. Nobody knew what to say. It was hard to hear, and I had so many questions. No one knew what to do. This was something you only see in movies.

For me to process something like that was really, really difficult. We were also told we weren't supposed to tell anybody, and we wanted to protect Jess. But at that point you have something that's traumatizing to someone special to you, but it was also traumatizing to us. Never having experienced it, I didn't know what to do with it.

We went home and luckily, my husband Bill was there, too. We're a close family, so he and I would talk about it, but it just left a void. I just sat there, and it would play in my mind. I wasn't there, and I didn't know exactly what happened to her. But I could imagine what happened to her. And then I got scared for her. I got sad for her. I got angry. I felt all kinds of emotions.

So then my sister Loretta and I went down to Chad and Jess's house the weekend after and went there just to be with Jess no matter what she wanted. Her strength wasn't there to take care of the kids, and mostly she might have needed to take a moment and go in a corner and cry. That was okay because the kids were taken care of. Chad was doing everything to take care of her, but we just went to be there.

You don't know how to support somebody. There's no handbook for this, and you can give her a hug. But you didn't want to pry. You wanted to be strong for her, but you wanted to be empathetic. It was really hard, and you could tell that she was different.

There was no emotion in her. It was like that had been stripped from her. She was hurting, but she was hollow. I wanted to talk, but we didn't know what questions to ask. And for me, my default is I love kids. I would try to be with the kids because I didn't know what else to say. I think it was the kids were so oblivious to it, and you feel that it's not something that should have impacted them. But unfortunately it does because they probably also knew that their mom was different and different things were happening.

We went to a bowling event with them. At one point I looked over at Jess, and it was like she was in a whole different place. There was so much action happening around us and it was almost like even if we talked her that she couldn't hear. She was just looking off into space. And I think I asked her if she was okay, and she didn't answer. I mean, how do you answer that after something like this has happened? And what questions do you ask? It was just strange. It was like watching somebody be a shell of themselves.

Sarah

As a close friend of Jessi's, I had been at Aria's birthday party, but I had left long before the assault happened. I've known Jessi since 2000, our freshman year of college at Northwest Missouri State University. We were roommates, and I was the maid of honor in her wedding. We're still best friends, so when the phone rang a few days after the assault, and it was Jessi, I wasn't worried.

But I'll never forget hearing about the rape for the first time. My first thought was, "What the fuck?" I couldn't wrap my head around what she was telling me. I still vividly remember the details she told me about her dad coming down the stairs. I didn't know what to say. What do you say to one of your best friends after she has been sexually assaulted? I had so many questions, but I didn't know if I should ask them. I just remember thinking, "Where does it go from here?" For months I would ask myself, "How does this happen?"

I hung up the phone, and I remember feeling so angry. What the hell was this person doing? And I thought about it a lot, not just in the immediate aftermath but throughout the years. I thought so much about how it affected her marriage and her role as a mother because her personal space had been traumatized.

At the time I was an ER nurse, and I always viewed rape in a clinical manner, but, damn, now my best friend has been through the same thing in her home, the place where you're supposed to feel the safest. Now, I relate differently to my patients. Before, it was just doing a job. Now, I have a better understanding of what it's like to go through that trauma.

Jessi

In the weeks, months, and even years after the assault, I was busy dealing with my own trauma. I wasn't concerned with how anyone else was dealing with what happened to me. It was all I could do to hold myself together, but I think it's worth taking a minute now to talk about secondary victims when it comes to sexual assault.

Sexual assault doesn't happen in a vacuum. Friends and family can also experience trauma related to the assault. It's one of the reasons so many marriages break up after an event like this. But many times, friends and family members don't think about seeking help for themselves. They convince themselves that because they weren't the ones who were assaulted that they did not experience the trauma. But the loved ones of a sexual assault survivor often are traumatized by the assault and often don't get the help that they need to process the trauma.

When I decided to write this book, I wanted to interview the important people in my life who were either there when it happened or who knew me in the immediate aftermath. As I conducted those interviews, I realized that many of my friends and family had been affected by what happened to me in ways that I had not anticipated, and many of them had never even thought about getting help for themselves.

Over and over again in these interviews, I heard how my friends and family simply felt helpless. They didn't know what to do for me, and, truthfully, I didn't know what I needed them to do for me. Many chose not to bring it up unless I brought it up. For many of my friends and family, they simply didn't talk about it at all for fear of feeling like they were gossiping about what happened. It's hard to know the right thing to do because I didn't want to know that people were talking about it. In fact, I asked my parents to keep it quiet until I was ready to speak. For many of my friends and family, keeping silent became a habit long after I was ready to tell my story, and I think it may have inhibited their ability to seek help.

Secondary victims of sexual assault deal with some of the same trauma as the rape victim when it comes to assigning blame and feeling responsible for not stopping the assault. In a study by Christainsen et al., 66% of survey respondents said they had thoughts about being able to prevent the assault.

Secondary victims also face trauma in being unable to help the primary victim after the assault. Understanding victims who are often in a dissociative state and dealing with their own trauma can leave loved ones feeling sidelined and as if their offers of help are being rejected. Nearly half of the respondents in the previously mentioned study said they were insecure about how to best help the sexual assault survivor, and 77% said they found supporting the survivor to be difficult. It is interesting to me that nearly two-thirds of survey respondents who were supporting a sexual assault survivor said they were satisfied with the support that they offered to the survivor.

Although the months after the rape are sometimes foggy in my memory, I do remember relying mostly on Chad and sometimes feeling as if everyone else just simply wanted to forget the rape had happened. I felt as if everyone expected me to simply return to being the person that I had been before because that would make it easier for everyone. People eventually stopped asking about it. The difference in perspectives and the separate but shared trauma of both sexual assault survivors and secondary victims makes the topic of how to support a sexual assault survivor more difficult than just sharing a checklist of things you should do for your friend or loved one after a sexual assault.

Not surprisingly, only a third of study respondents sought out help after being told of their loved one's sexual assault; however, nearly two-thirds of respondents said they needed help. This lines up with my experience. I asked each person I interviewed whether they had sought professional help after the attack, and only one person, my mom, had tried to get help. After a disappointing session with a therapist, she chose not to pursue any more counseling.

I wrote this chapter because secondary trauma is a real thing, and it can greatly impact the person experiencing the secondary trauma and their ability to help the sexual assault victim. The lack of understanding around secondary trauma can also keep friends and family from seeking the mental health help they need to be healthy themselves. Secondary trauma can result in some of the same long-lasting effects that sexual assault survivors themselves encounter, including PTSD, anxiety, and depression. Acknowledging the reality of secondary trauma can result in secondary victims getting the help they need even as they support the sexual assault survivor.

Jessi

As my friends and family started to process what had happened to me, I was still continuing to do the next thing on my list. That included seeing my primary care doctor. When I called to make an appointment, the receptionist told me they had no appointments available – until I told her why I needed to be seen. I immediately moved to the top of the list and they were able to squeeze me in that day.

When I went to my appointment, Chad went with me. My doctor had the same reaction as the receptionist. I'll never forget the look of pity and sadness on her face. She apologized for what had happened to me, but she wasn't the one who had anything to apologize for. After doing the exam and talking with me, she prescribed some medication for the constant nausea I was experiencing, but she couldn't do anything for my shattered soul.

The experience with my doctor's office is the perfect picture of life in the immediate aftermath of a rape, of the instant change in attitude any time you tell someone what happened. Whether it's the doctor's office or your best friend, the person's attitude immediately goes from normal or even indifferent to concern and, yes, pity. In an instant, the way people view you changes – you go from patient, friend, daughter, wife to rape victim and sexual assault survivor. While your perception of the world has changed so has people's perception of you. One of the biggest struggles of sexual assault survivors is fitting back into our lives when we are no longer the same people.

Those first few weeks after the assault are still a blur. Every moment was hard. Every day, I simply went through the motions. Every time I told someone what had happened, the whole thing became more real. I knew in every fiber of my being that I would never be the same person I was before. I would never be that cheerful, optimistic, life of the party woman again. I would always be looking over my shoulder, struggling to feel safe. Even now, after 11 years have passed and a lot of healing has taken place, arriving home to an open garage door because someone forgot to close it sends me into a panic. Who I am irrevocably changed on that day in November. It would take me a long time to come to terms with all that had been stolen from me – and I would need help.

My doctor recommended I see a psychologist, Dr. Susan Barngrover. I immediately called her but had to leave a message. When she called me back and I told her what I needed, she apologized that I had to tell her over the phone and quickly booked me an appointment for a few days later. When I walked into her office in downtown Lee's Summit, the only word that came to mind was old. The smell of old building assaulted my senses as I filled out paperwork in the small waiting room, the floor covered in '90s green carpet. When Dr. Barngrover welcomed me into her office I once again felt as if I had walked into a room the new millennium had forgotten. All my concerns about the dated decor fell away as my first session with Dr. Barngrover got underway. I almost immediately felt at ease as I walked her through my story, the telling of which would take most of our time. Her compassionate demeanor helped me through the trauma of retelling the events of that night yet again.

Finding a therapist you feel comfortable with and can trust in the wake of sexual assault can be difficult, but it is important to a survivor's healing to find someone who can help lead the way to healing. Therapists and psychologists have different approaches, different personalities, and different levels of understanding about sexual assault. A sexual assault survivor's path to healing often relies on having a good rapport with their therapist. You have to "click" because therapy must be a safe space to process the trauma that has happened. Unfortunately, not every sexual assault survivor is as lucky as I was to find that person on the first try. It's important to remember that it is okay to try out several different therapists or psychologists until the survivor finds the one that feels like a person who can help lead them to healing.

I was lucky that my doctor knew where to refer me for therapy and that Dr. Barngrover and I "clicked" on the first try. I didn't have to do any of the legwork to find a therapist for myself, but if you are looking for a therapist after sexual assault, the Rape, Abuse, and Incest National Network encourages rape victims to consider these three criteria:

1. The therapist should have experience with sexual assault.
2. The therapist's personality should be a good fit for yours.
3. Understand the type of therapy the therapist prefers. Some types of therapy require talking while others include more "homework." Understanding the therapy and thinking about what would work best for you is an important part of choosing a therapist.

Before I left my first session, Dr. Barngrover asked how I felt about Chad. Chad had become my world. I clung to him. I was afraid to be alone and wanted him by my side all the time. Dr. Barngrover told me that was a good sign because I believed that Chad would keep me safe, but she also told me that being intimate again would be on my timeline, that I would get to decide when I was ready. She wanted me to come back in two weeks and bring Chad or anyone else I felt comfortable bringing.

Chad

Not long after Jess had her first session, I went to see Dr. Barngrover by myself. I mostly needed to know that I was doing the right things to help Jess. Nothing prepares you for something like this, and I was determined that we were going to make it through this nightmare together. I wanted to be as prepared as I could be for anything that Jess might experience both at that time and in the future. Dr. Barngrover emphasized the need for Jess to be in control because that was what her rapist had stolen from her.

I was relieved to have her tell me that I was mostly doing the right things and had good coping mechanisms of my own in place to see me through. Healing doesn't happen overnight, and I needed to make sure I had all the tools I would need because I was in this for the long haul.

One thing I struggled with at the time, and still struggle with today is the fact that this happened while I was right there. She was in the next room, and I didn't know it was happening. I didn't stop it. I know others in our circle of friends and family have wondered why I didn't notice something was wrong, and some have even been angry at me for not doing anything. I will probably struggle with the weight of that for the rest of my life.

INTIMACY

"

When it came to my marriage, the assault actually played into one of my biggest fears: that our marriage would fall apart because of something that happened that I never got a chance to fix.

Jessi

Jessi

In addition to being an assault on your body and mind, sexual assault is a thief. In the beginning, in those first few weeks and even months after the assault, it felt like the rape had stolen everything from me.

A blog post from Johns Hopkins University does a better job of describing this than I can:

> Trauma, particularly the trauma of sexual and gender-based violence (GBV), also relies on abuse of power, manipulation, and exploitation. It is also a relentless thief. What does trauma tend to steal? It frequently targets your sense of safety, your ability to trust, and your view of the world. It might steal your view of yourself, your psychological and emotional well-being, or your concentration and focus. It takes your time (so much time) as well as all the things you could have spent your time on if it hadn't occurred. It often goes after your sense of autonomy, your relationship with your body, and your relationship with sexuality, including the ability to experience sexual pleasure even within the boundaries of

a safe, informed, and enthusiastically consented to sexual experience.

In my case, the assault stole all of those things, especially the last one. Physical intimacy after a sexual assault is difficult, no matter how you cope with the trauma. Studies show that between 71% and 88% of women who have been sexually assaulted say they have problems with sexual functioning after the attack. In addition, women who have been raped report "negative sexual effects, including more painful sex and reproductive health related medical issues." Sexual assault is not a one-time event that most women simply get over. It follows them into their bedroom for a long time, sometimes a lifetime.

When it happened to me, I wanted control back. I wanted my life back. I wanted the rape to not be at the center of everything. I wanted my marriage to be solid, and I didn't want to always see X's face when I thought about sex. Make no mistake, rape is not about sex. It's about power and control, and it doesn't qualify as sex by any definition. But the assault definitely makes sex afterward so much harder.

When it came to my marriage, the assault actually played into one of my biggest fears: that our marriage would fall apart because of something small that happened that I never got a chance to fix. It was an irrational fear before the assault that became even bigger after the rape. Because now something big had happened, and I wasn't in any shape to fix it. In addition, I felt like I was "damaged goods" because this guy had taken away the sanctity of my marriage.

A few weeks after the assault, I indicated to Chad that I thought I was ready to be intimate. It wasn't long before I was crying. Chad was concerned, but I didn't want to stop. Every time I closed my eyes, I saw HIS face, so I looked at Chad, so I could see, really see, how much he loved me and how much he wished he could take my pain away. In hindsight, Chad is the only one that could have ever gone through this with me. The whole time we were having sex, I felt like I was tainted. I kept having flashbacks, and I was angry that I was having flashbacks. Chad was so patient and concerned about whether he was hurting me either physically or emotionally.

Afterward, I lay in Chad's arms, and he just listened to me and let me cry. He made me feel safe and loved. Sex didn't get any easier for a while, but each time, I would cry a little less and eventually not at all. But it took months and months before I could finally close my eyes and not see my rapist's face looking down at me. Sex would eventually once again become an enjoyable part of my marriage but not without a lot of work and patience on the part of both Chad and me.

Chad

Being intimate was definitely not at the top of my mind after the assault. I was worried about Jess and trying to figure out how to help her through all of it. In addition, I was trying to process through what had happened and what it meant for all of us going forward. And I had my hands full trying to manage the kids and the household. It was a few weeks before we even tried to be intimate.

I remember asking her at least once and probably several times whether she was sure this was what she wanted to do and reassuring her that it wasn't something she *had* to do. I wasn't going anywhere, and we could take all the time she needed to be ready, but she was insistent that she wanted to make love. I'm not sure I'd call it that, though. That first time really felt like something she needed to do to work through all of the emotions, so she could separate the emotions from the act itself. It felt like she wanted to take back some control over what X had taken from her.

After that, we didn't make love for a while, and that was okay. Jess needed to focus on healing herself. I don't know how long it was before we were intimate again, but it was a slow process with some setbacks along the way.

Susan Barngrover, Ph.D.

My therapist, Dr. Barngrover, was key to my recovery, and I wanted to include some of her testimony from the civil trial to provide a clinical perspective on my mental state throughout my recovery and add some depth to the things I remember. – Jessi
(taken from the trial transcript)

Since the rape occurred, unfortunately, in her own bedroom, in her own bed, her bedroom took on all kinds of other triggers that you wouldn't expect. So she had to sleep in the bed in a certain way. She couldn't sleep on a certain side of the bed. When it came to sexual activities, certain touches, words, positions, all those things became no longer love-making, they became triggers for dissociation, so that it was hard for her to be intimate and vulnerable. A woman wants to be vulnerable with her husband, but it's hard to do after trauma.

Jessi

The calendar was not my friend when it came to the timing of the rape. The assault had happened over Thanksgiving weekend, which meant the Christmas holidays were coming. And that meant interacting with my family who love me but who also didn't know how to really help me. I was simply going through the motions of my life, not really taking an interest in anything, spending a lot of time dissociating. It was all I could do to get through a normal day. And the holidays are never normal.

I was barely beginning to come to the realization that I would never be the same person I had been before the assault ever again, but I was about to be forced into a situation where people would expect me to be that bubbly, happy, optimistic person that they knew. I didn't really know and certainly couldn't have expressed that that Jessi was gone. I felt like I died that day. There would be a new Jessi, a woman who had been through the fire and come out the other side, but she would not appear for a while. The Jessi that showed up in Omaha for Christmas Eve that year was traumatized, unsure, scared, and tired – so very tired.

So much of that holiday season I can't remember. It's just one more thing that X stole from me – the joy of the holiday season with young children. That's a Christmas I'll never recover and probably never remember anything more than snippets of. I do remember Christmas Eve at my parents' house. It was your typical big family gathering, with aunts and uncles, cousins and kids. Outside of the kids, everyone there knew what had happened to me. I knew they loved me. I knew they felt bad for me. But I also wondered, just as I wondered every time I told someone what had happened, whether they also judged me. I didn't want to feel that way, but I did.

I also felt like everyone just wanted me to be okay. It had been less than a month, but it seemed like the only way to make everyone else feel better was for me to feel better. And I didn't. I couldn't.

I was often one of the people involved in planning or executing the family games at our gatherings because I was the fun, creative one, the one who loved to smile and laugh. The family game was a tradition that started so many years ago that I can't even pinpoint the date. My mom bought the game Left/Right/Center, which we used as part of the secret Santa gift exchange. The next year, my mom asked me to write a Christmas-themed story to go with the Left/Right/Center game. From there, it evolved into what it had become that first Christmas after the assault – a full-fledged game show.

That year, the theme was The Price is Right. My mom had made the big price tag name tags and had games like Plinko. She wanted me to help her host, and everyone just expected that I would perform my normal role as the game master. But games were far from my mind. I agreed to do it, but I was nervous, a feeling I had never had around my family. All I could think about was how everyone would have their eyes on me. It made me feel like I had to perform not only as the game show host, but as if I had my shit together and that I was OK. I only have one memory during that game, and it was just standing up there, looking at the Plinko board feeling like I was simultaneously floating and going to be sick.

It wasn't just everyone's expectation that I would be fine. The whole holiday was overwhelming. In fact, at times, I could hardly stand to be around so many people. I remember one specific moment where I just had to get away. The party, the alcohol. It all just reminded me too much of the night of the assault. I went into the bedroom and sat on the floor, my back leaning against the bed and started sobbing uncontrollably. My Aunt Penny came in and simply sat down next to me and held me in her arms as I sobbed until I could barely breathe. At the time, the sobbing didn't bother me that much because it felt like a release, a letting go of something I had been holding in for a month. I don't know if my Aunt Penny said anything to me, but I do know that she came in and created a safe, comforting space for me to let my feelings out. Whether it was her training as a nurse or simply an instinct that her presence was more important than her words, on that Christmas Eve, she gave me exactly the gift I needed – someone willing to simply sit with me as I struggled in the darkness.

Looking back, it was probably all too much, too soon, but there is no instruction book for surviving sexual assault. You simply do the things you think you're supposed to do as you sort out who you are now, even if it's not who you think you want to be.

Josh

Even though I'm her brother, Jess and I weren't super close during the time period when the rape occurred. I actually didn't find out about it from Jess. My mom called to tell me what happened. Jess and I actually didn't have an in-depth conversation about it until a couple of years later, but that doesn't mean I didn't care. After I heard what had happened, I didn't know what to do. I asked my parents if I should go visit, but they didn't really think there was anything I could do. The first time I saw her was at Christmas, and she was just a different person. Definitely more reserved and not as bubbly. There were times she just didn't seem "with it." She was also jumpy and kind of on alert. Just not the Jess we all knew.

Mom/Debbie

I was so relieved to have Jess home for a few days. We hadn't seen her since the assault happened, and as a mom it always makes you feel better to be able to see your child, especially in a situation like this. I'll never forget Christmas Eve. I looked around and Jess was just gone; she had gone into the bedroom to be by herself. I didn't know what to do. I remember thinking, "Do I go in there and try to comfort her, or do I let her be alone and get through it herself again?"

I just didn't know how to react when these triggers happen. There's no experience to draw on, no parenting book to tell you how to manage this situation. No one taught me how to act when something like this happens. In hindsight, could I have gone and maybe gotten more counseling and better counseling to help me understand how to help her? Yes, but I didn't, and I can't change that.

And the situation compounded itself. After an incident like Christmas Eve, I would get scared because I didn't even realize things like a party could trigger a bad reaction for Jess.

Dad/Tony

It was great to have Jess home, but we didn't know how to act. We had called regularly to check on her, but it wasn't the same as seeing her. But it was hard to know how to act. I think we just tried to go on like nothing had happened, but Jess wasn't the same. The whole time she was there, it was like she was in a shell. She was just so traumatized by what had happened. We couldn't comfort her enough. We couldn't make it better. She was just so withdrawn, and that was hard.

Susan Barngrover, Ph.D.

Dissociation was a big part of my reaction to the trauma of the attack. It can be a difficult thing for those around you to understand. – Jessi

(taken from the trial transcript)

Nomenclature says that if you've been raped, that is our current statistical manual for diagnosis. Rape is automatically considered post-traumatic stress disorder. But from my training perspective also she met the criteria, the diagnostic care categories for PTSD. So she had to have experienced a trauma that was threatening to her, which she did, she was raped. Then also you have to have some re-experiencing of that phenomena, so that would be like flashbacks or dreams. There should also be some intrusive thoughts, which she had intrusive thoughts. Also there would be an avoidance so that a person would not want to talk about that or deal with anything that is associated with that. For example, triggers, certain triggers would set her off. Then we also have arousal, which would be -- not a sexual arousal, arousal of her HPA [Hypothalamic-Pituitary-Adrenal] axis, which would be the fight or flight or freeze response.

So when you have -- when you've been assaulted or you have a trauma, then your sympathetic nervous system is on most of the time. So your adrenaline is on, you're not able to be calm, not able to be relaxed. So she was choking a lot, gagging, because she couldn't get the words out, tearful, and would space off. Again, that inability to stay focused. So she was dissociative.

That's a term that we use in the diagnosis of PTSD. Dissociative means either you are not yourself, depersonalization or derealization that the seeing doesn't seem real. So it's almost a surreal feeling like you are a robot, autonomous where you are sort of disengaged from yourself and what is going on around you. And that is a coping mechanism, not one you chose, one that physiologically becomes like deer in the headlights, that kind of phenomenon. Also you would have negative connotations of things. So her world view had changed in that, you know, she believed that the world was a just place and that men protected women and this experience has changed that. So that fits that criteria of a huge alteration of one's perception of self in the world.

THE IMPORTANCE OF THERAPY

"

I don't think I would be alive without therapy.

Jessi

Jessi

By the time we left to go home after Christmas, I was exhausted from trying to pretend I was going to be okay. Christmas may be the season of hope, but that year, I was far from feeling hopeful. I had just started therapy and was deep in the dark hole of depression, simply trying to find my way from one day to the next, so I could find my way to recovery. I don't have the words to describe the deep darkness that covered me and stole my ability to care about anything. It would take years of work with my therapist and the right medication before I would fully finish the arduous climb out of the pit of depression and back into the light.

If I'm being completely honest and blunt, I don't think I would be alive without therapy. I had suicidal thoughts only once, but depression and anxiety leave you feeling lost and lonely. It feels like life will always be this way. The worst part of that time was feeling like no one understood. I still feel like if you've never been there, you don't get to have an opinion about how someone else should handle it. It's not something you can snap your fingers and make it go away.

During one visit, Dr. Barngrover encouraged me to search for and find my "happy place." I always go back to a small beach with pillowy soft sand that feels like it melts in between your toes and almost sparkles. I'm sitting in a lounge chair looking out at the water and all the beautiful shades of blue, but my favorite is the turquoise that is borderline green. I love watching the gentle waves in the distance and the way the water touches the shoreline of the beach. I envision the stark contrast of the stillness on top of the water and the vast sea life below. I can smell the salt in the air and the way the sun warms the sand and the air around me. When I get overwhelmed by all that happened to me, this is where I go.

Visualization like this is just one form of therapy, and it is something that works for me when I encounter a trigger. She also focused a lot of effort on skills to get the feelings out of my body. In addition to mental health disorders, sexual assault survivors are in danger of developing chronic health conditions such as diabetes, heart disease, hypertension, pulmonary disease, gastrointestinal disorders, and liver disease. We spent many sessions talking about various ways to channel my feelings like physical exercise, punching a pillow, or taking a baseball bat to an old piece of furniture. I also took medication for depression for a period of time. Dr. Barngrover was trying to help pull pieces together in a comprehensive whole, so I would be able to at least be able to identify triggers and emotions and have another way of looking at things, giving me some control over my experiences.

I also discovered that my environment could betray me in unexpected ways. Scents that seemed harmless to others, like a strong facewash, lotion, or perfume, could instantly drag me back into feelings I was not prepared to face. I threw out nearly every product I owned that carried a distinct smell and replaced them just to feel safe in my own skin. I began to understand how deeply tied I am to my senses. Learning that I am highly sensory became another piece of the puzzle in learning how to care for myself in the aftermath of the assault.

Every person is different, and what works for one person may not work for another. However, because of the prevalence of mental health issues in sexual assault survivors, finding something that does work for each person is crucial to healing and moving forward.

A majority of sexual assault survivors suffer from a mental health disorder after the attack, with the most common being depression, anxiety, and post-traumatic stress disorder. Outwardly, it may present as frequent mood swings, bouts of crying, irritability, short-temperedness, among other indications. These disorders are treatable, but it often takes a combination of therapy and medication – and a lot of hard work on the part of the survivor. Sexual assault isn't just one traumatic event; it's a lifetime of dealing with that trauma. Even when you've done the hard work to find the light on the other side of the darkness, the remnants of trauma can assault you at any time. It's just one more way that being a victim of sexual assault is so unfair. You live with the effects forever while the perpetrator often goes unpunished.

Therapy was part of that hard work for me, and my therapist was perfect for me. She was a woman of great faith, but she could also cuss like a sailor. She never called my rapist by his name; she simply called him motherfucker or son-of-a-bitch. She never made me feel tainted or less than and instead helped me understand and name what was happening to me, a crucial step in my healing process. Importantly, she helped me understand that sometimes what I was experiencing was just the normal process of being in a marriage and parenting two children. I mean, everyone is a bitchy mom sometimes, right? But that's what trauma does to you. It makes you unable to view the world through any lens but the one that trauma has created. Learning to not let trauma frame the way you see the world is just one part of the healing journey – and having the right therapist by my side was essential to learning that.

Susan Barngrover, Ph.D.

During the civil trial X's attorney tried to make Dr. Barngrover's use of the term son of a bitch an issue. This is her rationale for using that identifier for X. – Jessi
(taken from the trial transcript)

Q: So when you had your first visit with Ms. Bixler, you referred to..., my client, as a son of a bitch.

A. SOB, yes, sir.

Q. SOB means son of a bitch?

A. Yes, sir.

Q. And that's how you referred to him, as a son of a bitch and as a perpetrator, correct?

A. Yes, sir.

Q. That has been your standard line throughout your treatment of this lady; is that true?

A. Yes, sir, that's correct.

(our attorney's redirect examination)

Q. Tell the Judge why you referred to the defendant as an SOB.

A. Because stating the name of the perpetrator is extremely triggering, and I will not be able to really work with a patient if that's the case. So that's not what Jessica called him, that's what I called him because she had a hard time even saying what his name was, but that is extremely common. I'm trying to facilitate her anger at the appropriate person, which is the perpetrator, then I called him an SOB.

Jessi

Throughout this time, I began to start telling more people my story. It was important to me that I control who knew and what they knew so I could prepare myself for how they would react when I saw them. I had asked my parents to not tell anyone until I was ready. At one point, I found out my mom had told someone before I had said it was okay. That was difficult because this was my story. It had happened to me. And I wanted to be the one to control the narrative.

When you've been sexually assaulted, there is so much you can't control. It happens. You're traumatized. If you report it to the police, there are all these steps you have to go through that are pretty dehumanizing and completely out of control. Even when you finally get your day in court, so much of the outcome depends on people and evidence other than what you have to say. Telling or not telling people about the assault feels like one of the only things a sexual assault survivor can take ownership of, which is why it was so important to me to be the one to identify who could be told and when.

Telling people became this weird tug of war in my brain. When deciding who to tell, I was constantly worried. How would they react? Would they judge me? What would they say? Would they understand? But while I was worried about them judging me, I became aware that I was judging everyone's reactions when I told them. I couldn't have articulated what I thought the perfect reaction would be, but I definitely judged when it wasn't what I thought it should be.

People have all different reactions when they are told about a rape. Some want to smother you with love and sympathy. Others hear what you have to say, make a comment about how sorry they are then want to move on. Most people just simply don't know what to say. They don't know how or if they should bring it up in future conversations. As a survivor in the midst of healing, it was almost impossible for me to tell people what I needed from them, so everyone was left to muddle through the conversation as best they could.

When we were home for Christmas, I decided we could tell Chad's best friend, Dan, and his wife, Nancy. Dan and Chad had been college roommates, and I met them at Chad's sister's wedding, which was our third date. We had all been good friends ever since. While we were in Omaha, Dan and Nancy brought their kids over to my parents' house to play with the other kids. We took the opportunity to speak with them alone in the living room upstairs. I learned later that Nancy was worried that we were going to tell them I had cancer. I don't remember exactly what was said, but their response was loving and compassionate. Nancy immediately came to sit beside me and hold me while Dan expressed how sorry he was that the assault had happened and told us they would be there for whatever we needed. He also told me he was unlikely to bring it up again because he didn't want to unintentionally trigger something for me but that they would always be there for us.

Their response meant everything to me. It was one of the first times that I told my story that I didn't feel like the people I was telling were judging me. I never wondered what was going through their heads, and I never felt as if they were pitying me. I felt loved and supported, and it was such a relief.

At some point, I decided to tell my friend Jill, who had been one of my college housemates and the maid of honor in our wedding. Jill is my eternally optimistic friend, and I had put off telling her what had happened because I was afraid she would want to push me to look on the bright side of things. I finally called her on my way home from work one day and explained why I had been so distant for so long. I had avoided talking to her because she was my "rainbows and butterflies" friend and that wasn't what I thought I needed at the time. She expressed her sorrow for what had happened, and I apologized for not calling her sooner. When I finished telling her, she said, "I'll let you go." I was shocked. I was ready to talk, and it seemed that one of my closest friends couldn't wait to get off the phone with me. It wouldn't be until I interviewed her for this book that I would find out she thought I was just calling to explain and that I didn't want to talk about it more.

Relationships can be difficult when everything in your life is going well. Even then, we can unintentionally hurt people. Throw in sexual assault, dissociative states, healing from trauma, friends trying to do the right thing without any help figuring what the right thing is, and it's a recipe for fracturing relationships and strengthening others. No matter how people deal with being told about a sexual assault of someone they love, there's never going to be a perfect response. How the survivor perceives the response may be completely the opposite of what the friend or relative intended and vice versa. This is just another one of the many unexpected consequences of being sexually assaulted. One more way that life unfairly becomes immensely more difficult. And one more thing everyone has to muddle their way through, doing the best they can with the tools and information they have at the time.

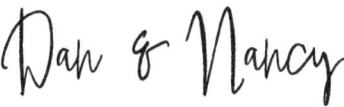

Dan

We were at Jess's parents' house, and our four-month-old was being cranky. Jess's mom offered to take her, but I kept telling her no. She finally said something that had me handing her over, and we went with Chad and Jess upstairs to the living room. We thought they were going to tell us they were getting divorced or that someone was sick. Rape never crossed our minds.

We don't remember exactly what was said, but our first reaction was to figure out what we could do. I quickly realized that there wasn't much to be done other than to listen to them and to love them. I also said that I would probably never bring it up again but not to mistake my silence for not caring.

Nancy

My dad had just passed away a couple of weeks before, and I know they were apprehensive about telling us. I was heartbroken for both Jess and Chad. I wanted them to know that we loved them and would be there for them, but I didn't know what to say. We were heartbroken, and I remember being a little bit mad at Chad that this had happened. I wasn't sure how Jess would ever recover from this.

I had questions, but I definitely wasn't comfortable asking them that night. I do remember wondering about them being intimate and how much of a hurdle that would be to get over. I know we felt honored that they trusted us with their trauma, and we wanted to do anything we could to help.

Jill

I think Jessi texted me a short text to tell me what had happened not long after it happened, but then I couldn't get in touch with her. I would call and she wouldn't answer or return my calls. I worried that I had done or said something to upset her. When she finally did call me back, I was so relieved to hear from her.

When she called, she said something like, "I'm not mad at you, but you are my friend that will be like rainbows and butterflies about stuff." And she said, "I just didn't need that right at that moment. I love you, but I just needed somebody probably more to listen versus trying to find a blanket or to be like, 'Oh, are you okay?'"

It wasn't hurtful because that's what I tried to be to my friends. But when she told me what had happened, I just didn't want to pry. I got uncomfortable and didn't know what to say. I just felt like she would tell me what she wanted to tell me, and I didn't want to bring it up and make everything heavy. I didn't want to be nosy and make everything weird.

DISSOCIATION

> So her smart brain, her frontal lobe is not working, only her emergency system is on. And when your emergency system is on and you've been raped, typically you freeze more than fight or flight.

Susan Barngrover, Ph.D.

Jessi

Having gone back to work and made it through the holidays, I may have looked like I was on the road to healing, but in reality, so little time had passed, and I still had a long way to go on my healing journey, which became abundantly clear in January 2014. My company was hosting a sales meeting in Jamaica, and Chad and I had decided to go a few days early. We went all out on our stay, choosing a room at a boutique resort with a 180-degree view of the ocean. When we walked into our room, I immediately began unpacking my belongings on the side of the bed farthest from the door, which I still do to this day. We even had our own personal butler. It should have been wonderful. And it was until the night we decided to go to the bar/lounge area after dinner.

I settled into a lounge chair with a view of the ocean while Chad went to get our drinks. He ran into someone he knew and while he was only out of my sight for five to ten minutes, he was gone longer than I expected him to be. Out of nowhere a feeling of floating crept up on me. I was sitting in the chair, gripping the arms, my eyes staring blankly without blinking. I had no idea my body was frozen. It was as if I was observing my physical self. I was fully aware that there was music playing in the background and I was sitting in a chair, but I was not aware that my body was frozen and my eyes hadn't blinked.

When Chad returned, he said, "Jess?" and I snapped out of it. When I came to, my whole body was tingling like when one of your limbs falls asleep. My hands were sore from gripping the arms of the chair so tightly. I immediately began crying and shaking and asking Chad why he had left me. To me, the entire episode felt like it had taken hours when only a few minutes had passed.

When I met with Dr. Barngrover, I learned that I needed to start grounding myself in the present whenever the feeling of floating would start to overtake me. The body copes with trauma in a multitude of ways. Dissociating from your present experience when it becomes overwhelming is one of those ways. In Jamaica, Chad leaving combined with the lights and the music had overwhelmed my brain's ability to process it, leaving me "floating." Dr. Barngrover taught me how to return to myself by focusing my attention on something concrete, often related to my senses, to improve my feeling of stability and safety. For example, I could tell myself "I'm sitting in this chair" and physically hold onto the arms of the chair and look at my hands while thinking about how it feels and what I smell around me.

The truth about trauma of any kind is that it doesn't just go away. You simply learn how to deal with it and work through it. Even today, 12 years and a lot of work later, there are still things that can trigger a fight or flight response that require that I use the grounding skills I learned in the months after the assault. Working through trauma from sexual assault isn't like healing from surgery. You can't just follow the doctor's instructions for six weeks and go back to living your life the exact same way you did before. The trauma will always be there. I will always have moments that I have to work through. Thanks to X, living a life untouched by trauma is no longer an option for me. But choosing to move forward and take each day as it comes is a choice that I make every day because for me, if I don't try to move forward and work through my trauma when those moments come, then I let X take even more from me than he already stole. And for me, that would be unacceptable.

Chad

While those first weeks were really difficult trying to find our way to a place where Jess could function, it didn't really get much easier in the months that followed. Jess would often be in a dissociative state, and I was just trying to make sure both she and the kids had everything they needed. It was hard to know what to do for Jess.

I wasn't always sure whether she needed space or if she needed to leave for a bit or if I needed to lean in or take the kids away. Sometimes, she needed us to be around, but other times she would need time to be with her friends. There was no way of really knowing. You just kind of got a feeling and had to go with it. Sometimes, I would use my sales experience and ask her questions like "What do you feel about this or what do you think about this?" or "Suppose we decided to do this, how would that make you feel." I tried not to ask direct questions like "What if you came to this?" That often didn't turn out so well.

Figuring out how to help Jess was a process of trial and error that we both had to feel our way through without a lot of help, but I was determined to be there for her and provide the support she needed.

Susan Barngrover, Ph.D.

Understanding what is happening when someone is in a dissociative state can help loved ones of a sexual assault survivor offer support and know how to approach different situations.
– Jessi
(taken from trial transcript)

From a medical perspective your sympathetic nervous system is on that fight or flight or freeze response. So when she dissociates, there is usually a trigger, she may not be aware of what that is, but usually a trigger will cause you to do that, either something, an external cue, will cause that or an internal feeling will cause that, and she may not be aware of that. And then her body and mind work in concert to shut out anything. So her smart brain, her frontal lobe is not working, only her emergency system is on. And when your emergency system is on and you've been raped, typically you freeze more than fight or flight. So she's there but you have to kind of get her attention.

Jessi

In the weeks following the assault, I found myself searching for ways to cope. The pain was everywhere. It lived in my body, in my thoughts, in the quiet moments and the crowded ones. How do you cope with the unthinkable? Nothing in my life had prepared me for the devastating physical and mental consequences of sexual assault. Everything felt out of my control. I felt broken, and I wasn't sure I would ever put the pieces back together.

I knew I needed something—anything—that could help me feel like I was still here, still whole. I decided to return to a hot vinyasa flow yoga class I had been regularly attending on Sunday evenings.

Just over a week after the assault I stepped into the familiar studio, the warmth of the room wrapping around me. I even found my usual spot—back corner, third row—but nothing felt normal. My hands trembled as I rolled out my mat. I was terrified, but I couldn't have told you why. I had done this exact routine for months, but that night, everything was different. I felt like the class participants could somehow see what had happened to me.

The instructor dimmed the lights and started the music, and I started crying, a steady stream that fell throughout the entire class. My body moved through the poses, but emotionally I was unraveling. I didn't know how to hold what was surfacing. By the time we reached shavasana, the part of class meant for rest and stillness, I felt anything but peaceful. Lying there, eyes closed, arms open, I felt exposed—vulnerable in a way that felt almost dangerous. I tried to focus, to breathe, to be still. But I couldn't. My body was there, but the rest of me was scattered in pieces.

Still, I kept going back.

Something about the repetition, the structure, the permission to move and feel without words—it gave me space to exist. To process. To heal, even if just a little at a time. Over the weeks that followed, I began anchoring myself with a mantra: I am strong. At first, it felt like a lie. I was anything but strong; I was barely making it through each day. But I said it anyway. Over and over, as I held each pose, as I sat in silence, as I tried to steady my breath. I am strong. I am strong. I am strong.

Eventually, I started to believe it.

I learned to visualize myself on a beach—feet in the sand, breeze on my face—inviting calm to wash over me like the tide. I practiced breathing through the anxiety, through the fear. I began to reconnect with my body, to reclaim it and feel that it was mine again.

A few weeks later, I signed up for an all-day yoga retreat. I asked my friends Sarah and Ashley to come with me, and they didn't hesitate. That day, we explored new styles of yoga, listened to teachings I hadn't been exposed to before, and spent quiet time together. At lunch, a speaker talked about empowerment and how it lives in the choices we make, the ways we show up for ourselves, even when it's hard.

Her words were soft, but they hit me like a wave. I couldn't tell you everything she said, only that it felt like she was speaking directly to me. Sarah took my hand, and just like that, the tears returned. But this time, the tears weren't about what was taken from me, they were about recognition, about feeling seen.

Another speaker talked about gratitude journaling, and something about it resonated. I had never kept a journal before. Writing wasn't a way I expressed myself, especially not my pain. The speaker suggested starting small, simply writing down three things a day that I was thankful for. Not the big stuff. Just tiny, quiet pieces of joy: the smell of fresh-cut grass, the sound of kids laughing, the warmth of a sunbeam through the window. I thought I could do that. And it was worth trying.

What I didn't expect was how much it would change me. Naming those little moments helped me feel more rooted in the present. It gave me glimpses of goodness in the middle of so much darkness.

Another light in the darkness was when my co-worker introduced me to the concept of "body work." I thought she was talking about going to see a massage therapist, but she quickly corrected me, explaining that while there were similarities, body work was different, with its own training and certifications. She caught my attention when she told me that most people hold stress and trauma in their bodies, but where it lives depends on the experience. She said women who have endured sexual trauma often carry it in their shoulders and even more commonly in the hips and pelvic region. Research supports this: studies have shown that trauma survivors, especially women, are more likely to experience chronic tension, restricted movement, and even pain in these areas as the body attempts to "store" what the mind cannot fully process. Some people feel an immediate release when that tension is worked through; others may never notice an improvement, but the work still matters.

As a courtesy to my friend, and with a vow to continue making progress in my healing, I agreed to talk with her partner who was certified in body work. Later that afternoon I phoned her partner, asked about her approach, and felt at ease almost immediately. We scheduled a session for that Friday, the same day my mom was arriving.

When I pulled into the driveway around 4:30, I was nervous but determined. My co-worker's partner opened the door with a firm handshake and invited me to sit at her kitchen table. She explained that she liked to spend the first thirty minutes simply getting to know her clients, listening to their stories and asking questions that might reveal where the body held tension. I told her what had happened to me, and she trusted me enough to share parts of her own story in return. She then showed me to the bathroom and led me to the therapy room, a warm space with a massage table, framed certificates, photos, and small bottles of essential oils.

I slid beneath the blanket on the table and waited. She knocked gently before entering, then explained each step before she began. Throughout the session she stayed connected, noting when certain areas of my body tensed as I spoke about painful memories. I cried, I shook, I felt waves of anger, and then I felt something shift. For the first time I experienced what it was like to release some of the weight I had been carrying. I felt understood, not alone, and for a moment I believed I didn't have to keep holding all of this pain inside.

When the session ended, she placed a smooth red stone shaped like a heart in my hand. She told me she sensed how strong I was, but she also knew there were more trials ahead. "Keep this with you," she said. "When it feels too heavy, hold it and remember what is already inside of you."

I drove the forty-five minutes home in a haze, my body drained and heavy, my mind still spinning. When I walked in the door, Chad and my mom met me with watchful eyes and quiet anticipation. They knew where I had been and wanted to know how it went, but they also gave me space. I curled up in the corner of the couch and shared what I could, though exhaustion weighed me down. I caught myself staring into the distance, a mirror of the blankness that had worried them so many times before. But this time was different. I reassured them that I only needed time and quiet to process.

Susan Barngrover, Ph.D.

(taken from the trial transcript)

Then I worked with Jessi on what her coping skills are, and what she's like as a person. She's very bright, she's articulate, she's always been pro-community, that kind of a person. So that we could use those strengths to help her transform that rape experience into something that does not bring up medical problems for the rest of her life.

That's my experience and that's what the data shows, that that will cause physiological problems. So then what we work on is she comes in and we talk about some triggers, some things that are bothering her. She has been doing yoga, we talk about breathing, we talk about visualization. She's very good at visualization. And ways to transform that experience so she has some control over how she processes it.

She didn't have any control over what happened but she can have control over that. And then try to normalize that, that the things she's feeling and experiencing are what you would expect from a rape survivor.

Jessi

By the spring of 2014, I was still trying to do "normal" things. Our friends Dan and Nancy came to town, and we decided to go to a Kansas City Royals baseball game.

At one point, Chad got up to go to the bathroom, so I grabbed my phone and started scrolling through Facebook. A picture came up on my feed, and my stomach dropped. All the breath left my lungs. Staring at me from my phone was my attacker's smiling face alongside another one of Chad's cousins and his family of five. Everyone in the photo was smiling and had their arms around each other. The shock and betrayal was immediate.

I entered a semi-catatonic state, immobilized and blankly staring ahead. I could hear Nancy calling my name, but her voice was muffled as if she were trying to speak underwater. She eventually broke through my stupor and I was able to show her my phone. Dan and Nancy contacted Chad who hurried back. But there would be no more pretending to have a normal, fun day for me. We immediately left the game.

For the court system, the public, and friends and family, more than nearly any other crime, rape often boils down to which person's story they believe more. Many people think that sexual assault is a crime committed by strangers, but the truth is that 80 percent of sexual assaults are committed by someone the victim knows, which means those in the victim's circle of friends and family often also know the attacker. This sets up a scenario where those friends and family are forced to decide who they believe, with sometimes devastating results for the survivor.

This is what I believed had happened with Chad's cousin. I didn't understand how they could choose to hang out with X – and post a photo of it – knowing what he had done to me. Seeing that photo made me feel like no one believed me. Chad's cousin had a teenage daughter of his own. How could he not be scared to have his wife and daughter around X? It seemed as if everyone else had chosen to carry on as if nothing had happened, but I was simply struggling to keep my head above water.

The next day Chad reached out to his cousin's wife who had posted the photo and had an angry conversation with her. I wasn't part of the conversation, but I know he told her he never wanted to speak to her or her husband again if they were siding with my attacker. We both unfriended them on Facebook that day. Chad's cousin's wife sent a text to Chad's mom saying that she had removed the photo, but the damage had been done. It wasn't about the picture; it was about the intent. They knew what X had done, and they still chose to be around him.

Chad

Before the attack, we were close to my extended family in the way that you are close to people you see a couple of times a year, but after the assault, we didn't go to many large family events because we couldn't be sure X wouldn't be there. And after the incident with the Facebook photo, it felt like some of my family just wanted us to move on, and I don't necessarily blame them.

It's hard. Until you actually go through it, it's typical human nature to say, "Oh well, that would never happen to me." It created distance between us and some of our friends and family. Walking through the aftermath of sexual assault isn't like healing from a broken leg. There's no defined end date for when everything should be better. And there's no guarantee everything will get better.

That's maybe one of the reasons why we have all different friends now, too, because you have to find people that have the kind of empathy that will sit with you in the darkness, no matter how long it lasts. The attack flushed out a lot of surface relationships but also let us know who our true friends were.

PROSECUTION

"

I can't prove that he intentionally came into your bedroom to rape you.

Jackson County Prosecutor

Jessi

"I'm not going to press charges."

I don't think I will ever forget hearing those words from the prosecutor's mouth. Nor will I ever forget the stunned silence that followed. My brain seemed unable to process the words. Disbelief didn't even begin to describe it.

From the night of the assault, Chad and I had done everything we could to hold X accountable, and the detectives had asked us if we wanted to prosecute. I thought I got to choose. I had gone through the trauma of the exam at the hospital. We had given our statements. I had gotten a restraining order. But the wheels of justice move slowly, and as we would soon find out, sometimes not at all.

We had done all the right things to press charges, so when we decided to go ahead and do that, we met with the prosecutor. My main concern was making sure X never had the opportunity to do this again. When we met with the prosecutor, she told us the first step was to process the rape kit and then X could be charged with rape or sexual assault, meaning if he was found guilty, he would be on the sex offender list.

I had the rape kit done on Dec. 1. It was February 19 before the prosecutor even requested that the rape kit be processed. After that, I would check with the prosecutor's office via email and was consistently told they were waiting for the rape kit to come back. The waiting was the worst part. I just kept thinking about the horror stories I had heard about rape kits not being processed. I didn't know anything about how the justice system worked, and I was getting increasingly concerned that we would run out of time to file charges. I felt like we were always bugging the police and the prosecutor, persistently asking where things stood and what our next steps were. It wasn't until June that the results of the rape kit finally came back.

The prosecutor's office told us to come in and meet with the prosecutor. I was nervous but determined, finally ready to hear how X would be arrested and charged. I knew the trial process would be difficult, but I wanted to see justice done.

The decision to pursue prosecution is a difficult one for any sexual assault survivor. Some studies have found that more than 60 percent of rape victims never report the assault to the police. Some choose not to report because they are afraid of not being believed. Others don't want to undergo the trauma of a trial. Those that do choose to prosecute often never see the offender incarcerated.

Chad and I walked into the prosecutor's office that day with no thought of not prosecuting the case. X had assaulted me in my own home. Other people had seen the aftermath. We had DNA evidence that it had happened. In my mind, this was an open and shut case.

When we entered the office, there was a woman there from one of the local non-profits. I thought she was there to help us, but she wasn't much help at all. In fact, it felt like she was just there to witness the meeting. She never said anything and didn't do anything to make us feel at ease. We all sat down in the prosecutor's office, and she said those words: "I'm not going to press charges."

Chad and I finally recovered from the shock and began asking questions. The most important being, "Why not?"

"Because I can't prove intent."

I didn't even know what that meant. The man had climbed into my bed and assaulted me while I was asleep. How much more intent do you need?

"I can't prove that he intentionally came into your bedroom to rape you."

Chad brought up the DNA evidence, but the prosecutor again told us that didn't prove intent.

I didn't know what to think. Was she accusing me of some complicity in my own assault? Why did this woman not think she could win this case? Reality started to blur. The room spun. My vision dimmed, and I experience the floating sensation of dissociation. I couldn't breathe. None of this made sense. I thought I got to choose whether to prosecute. This happened to me. It was my life X had destroyed. Why didn't I get a say in the process? Why did someone else get to decide?

We continued to question her, but we never got a clear answer of what she would need to prove intent. And then she said the words that will forever be seared into my memory.

"I want you to know I believe you."

I stared at her, thinking "Are you fucking kidding me?"

You, a complete stranger and someone who is charged with upholding the law and keeping criminals off the street, believe me? I never asked you what your opinion was. And is that supposed to give me comfort?

If anything, it did the opposite. I was now just one of the majority of sexual assault survivors whose attacker would never pay for what he did. The statistics are not in favor of sexual assault survivors ever getting justice through the legal system. According to RAINN (Rape, Abuse and Incest National Network), just 310 of every 1,000 rapes are reported to police, or just 31 percent. And those cases have a small chance of leading to a criminal conviction – or even making it to trial. A 2019 study by three University of Massachusetts-Lowell researchers found that just 7 percent of cases resulted in a conviction. In fact less than 1% of the cases in their study were resolved by a jury trial, meaning nearly all of them never entered a courtroom. The study highlighted the fact that most sexual assault cases never see the light of day because prosecutors don't want to litigate a case they aren't sure they can win – even when the police think they have a solid case – which is exactly what happened to my case.

We left the prosecutor's office without shaking hands or saying goodbye. We got in the car, and I started dry-heaving, my one shot at holding my attacker accountable, at seeing him pay for his crime, gone because one woman decided she wasn't willing to try to prove my case in court because it might hurt her office's conviction rate.

Across the country, city and county prosecutors are elected officials. They have to campaign every four years to retain their job, which makes them more politician than lawyer. Low conviction rates can lead to them losing their jobs, so many times, they choose not to prosecute cases they are not sure they can win – even if solid evidence exists. Sexual assault crimes are difficult to prove. They often come down to who is most believable on the witness stand – the victim or the accused. Rarely, are they a slam dunk win, so elected prosecutors may shy away from them for fear too many losses will hurt their conviction rate. In fact, our civil lawyer told me later that during the time of my case, the prosecutor's office had a policy that they would only prosecute cases that had a 97-99% chance of conviction. I was just one of many crime victims who would never get a chance to see justice.

Chad

When the prosecutor said she couldn't prove intent, I thought she was crazy. I remember saying, "So you are telling me if I had video of Jess going to bed, him walking into our room and committing the crime, you STILL wouldn't have enough to prosecute?"

And the prosecutor looked at me and said, "No. Because the video doesn't show what took place prior and doesn't represent his motives."

We left the office, and I was angry, but my biggest concern was for Jess. She had just had the rug pulled out from under her, and there was no way to fight the decision. The prosecutor was the only person who could make the decision to charge X. We had no say. I guess we were just supposed to accept this and move on with our lives, but what did that even look like? Once again, there was no playbook for this situation.

We got back to the car, and Jess started dry-heaving and punching the dashboard, screaming, "I don't understand! How can this be happening?"

The months after the assault had been so hard, but knowing that eventually Jess would get her day in court kept us going. Now, that had been ripped away. We felt let down. We had put our faith and trust in the system and had had that taken away. We didn't know what to do next. In the aftermath, Jess continued to have dissociative episodes, and we struggled to keep moving forward.

Susan Barngrover, Ph.D.

After the revelation that the prosecutor was not going to prosecute, I went to see Dr. Barngrover. In court, our attorney asked her to explain why this decision was so devastating to me.
– Jessi
(taken from the trial transcript)

Q: Did you also see Jessi when there was – apparently the prosecuting office decided not to prosecute?

A. Yes, sir.

Q. Did that have an impact on her at that time?

A. Yes, sir.

Q. Tell us about that.

A. Partly because Jessi is a very upright person and she is moral and believes that there's justice in the world and it will be served. That really set her back, because since the prosecuting attorney didn't follow through with that, that damaged her belief in a just world. So that's what you would expect, because she was hoping that he would be prosecuted, he would go to jail, and then he would be known as somebody who was a danger to women and she felt like she would be serving her community and protecting other people from a similar fate.

Jessi

I was beyond devastated by the prosecutor's decision, but just as I quickly learned after my attack, life has to go on. My kids still needed a mom. My husband still needed a wife. My job still needed an employee. But I didn't want to do any of those things. I was already struggling to continue putting one foot in front of the other, and the lack of prosecution felt like a huge betrayal weighing down everything. This horrible thing had happened to me, and now the man who did it would just walk away?

As I struggled to process this, I continued to struggle both at home and at work. After I returned from our Jamaica trip, I began having trouble meshing with my boss. We had previously been close, but the trauma of the attack had changed our dynamic. I had always tried to maintain positive interactions with my boss and my co-workers, but I found myself in the middle of conflict time and time again. That summer, I made the decision to look for a new job.

In the fall, I started a new job with a company out of Texas. My friend and coworker John (he was the first person at the office I told about the rape) had taken a job with this company, one of our largest customers. After starting his position, he realized the company desperately needed a new website and some marketing help, which was my area of expertise. The company flew me to Texas, wined and dined me. A couple of months after our first meeting, they offered me a job, which I accepted.

I started my new job in mid-September, and I decided to make my office the basement room where X and his wife were to have slept on that night almost a year ago. I wanted to reclaim this place in my home. I was tired of letting the assault define how I felt about my own home, this house that Chad and I had built to be our dream home. Setting up my office with the monitors and computers the company had sent me helped to heal just a few of the broken pieces inside of me.

But make no mistake, I was still broken. I still had dissociative episodes. Fear was still an everyday companion. I was grumpy for no reason. I would snap at Chad, snap at the kids. And so much of the world was just overwhelming. Chad and I would get into arguments because he would get upset when I would yell at the kids. Somewhere inside me, I knew that I wasn't being the best version of myself, but this was the only version I could be right now. I needed more time to crawl out of the dark.

I do remember one day when I was laying in the living room in a dissociative state. I don't know how many times my son had called my name before it penetrated the fog. He started walking down the stairs toward me, and I pulled the blanket up to my chin, wanting to hide from my own child. But my son was not deterred. He climbed up on the chaise with me and snuggled against me, not saying anything. After a few moments, he said, "Mommy, if you are scared, don't worry, I'll protect you."

And even though in that moment I felt weak and scared, I accepted what had happened to me. It wouldn't be that day, it wouldn't be that month, but I knew that eventually I would walk out of the fog, that I would overcome what had happened to me – because a sweet, innocent little boy needed a mom who could help him grow into the person he was destined to be.

Jessi

One thing I've noticed since the attack is that nobody talks about the fear. Or the sadness. Or the anger. The thing about all those emotions is that you can't take them out on the person who did this horrible thing to you. So you take it out on the people around you.

In the beginning, I was always afraid. I couldn't stand to be separated from Chad. When I entered a room, I always looked to make sure X wasn't there. It was irrational. He didn't live here. The likelihood that he would be in any room I was in on a random day was pretty much zero. But that didn't matter. I didn't feel safe.

Fear isn't something that's easy to get over. Most of us know that common spiders aren't going to hurt us, and are, in fact, good at getting rid of pests like mosquitoes, but that doesn't matter when your fear response kicks in. All you want to do is get away from it. And that's what I wanted – to get away from anything that could possibly harm me.

Fear also fed my anger. I would get so angry at people, especially my family members when they would ask me generic questions like "How are you doing?" I just kept thinking, "How do you think I am doing? I'm barely hanging on, and I'm scared every second that my life is falling apart and that my kids won't have a mother anymore, among a million other things.

As I've said before, I would also target Chad and my kids with my anger. The littlest things would set me off into a fit of raging anger. Again, this is a normal reaction for trauma survivors, but it can destroy the very relationships that are so important to healing.

And then there's the sadness, the grieving for all that you have lost – your sense of safety, your sense of justice, your sense of self. You were violated in the worst way possible, and the world around you doesn't really give you time to grieve or rebuild yourself. So, you try to tuck it away, try not to be overwhelmed by the sense of grief and desolation that seems to have permanently invaded your world.

As we moved forward after the decision not to prosecute, I found myself wallowing in all of these feelings. It felt like much of the progress I had made was gone. I didn't know what to do next. I didn't know what to feel or how to heal. Life doesn't pause because you are trying to figure out how to heal after being raped. Too often, just when you feel like you are making progress, life gives you a swift punch in the throat.

Susan Barngrover, Ph.D.

It wasn't just my struggle to "get over" what had happened to me that made me sad, angry, and irritable. My body's response to stress and fear had been irrevocably changed. – Jessi
(taken from the trial transcript)

Physiologically by having a trauma you have changed the person forever physiologically. The HPA [Hypothalamic-Pituitary-Adrenal] axis will tend to kick up the adrenal glands, you will be set at a higher rate so that you will be typically much more irritable, you'll have sleep disturbance, you'll be much more weepy. Your brain is now set for trauma and so you're not able to always access your smart and reasoning brain.

Chad

After the prosecutor's decision, we continued to just simply do the best we could to make it through each day. That entire first year was hard. Jess was so closed off and distant. Sometimes she would just stay in bed and not come out to talk to any of us. Too often she simply wore a blank stare, ignoring the kids tugging on her shirt asking her questions.

She was so angry, uncontrollably angry. She would get overly upset if one of the kids left something out, yelling and screaming. Then she would just close herself off and become distant again. It was like walking through a minefield every day.

It made it hard to do the little things, like come up behind her and give her a hug or a peck on the cheek. I was always thinking, "how is she going react? If I put my arm around her, is this going to set something off?" It could be the littlest thing like accidentally bringing up one of my relatives in conversation that could link to X or his wife.

I worried a lot – about our quality of life, about how our immediate family would survive. I also worried about the future. How would our daughter react when she eventually found out what happened on her birthday. I worried that I wouldn't be able to hold our family together. I didn't know if I could provide Jess with the support she needed, and I was really concerned Jess wouldn't be able to provide the support our kids would need from their mother.

And now that the option to prosecute X was off the table, I didn't know what to expect next. I was dealing with my own anger, but I needed to be there for Jess and the kids. I was happy she had found a new job, but I wondered if working from home was the right thing. This house that we had loved so much was often just a reminder of the horror of that night, and now she would be working in the same room where X and his wife had been. This home that we had loved so much at times felt like a prison. It was just another instance where it felt like every step through the minefield our lives had become could set off an explosion we might not recover from.

Susan Barngrover, Ph.D.

All of my fear, anger, and sadness were part of my PTSD, which our attorney asked Dr. Barngrover to describe for the court.
– Jessi
(taken from the trial transcript)

Q. Now, as you're going through the course of this treatment, does she have issues with anger?

A. Yes. I would call it irritability, sir.

Q. Okay. And so describe for us what you mean by that.

A. Jessi reports that she is more irritable with her children than she would like to be. Again, if you're set up on a very high physiological response where you're easily stressed already and have an exaggerated sorrow response, that's part of PTSD, then it doesn't take as much for you to lose your patience. So she's more irritable and has less patience with her children. Part of the hallmark of trauma treatment is to take the anger and put it towards the perpetrator and not toward yourself or people that don't deserve the anger.

Q. Does she have issues as it relates to depression?

A. Yes, sir. She frequently cries, most of the time she comes to see me she is tearful and chokes up, that trying to restrict that affect because it's overwhelming. And she's sad and she's weepy and at times have felt hopeless, not so much anymore but in the beginning definitely.

Q. What about fear?

A. Yes, she's afraid. I saw when she came in she made sure she sat there and her husband sat between her and him [X]. So she's afraid. That's common what you'd expect with trauma, always looking over your shoulder, always expecting someone to hurt you, because again, her world view is that men were chivalrous, protectors, they looked out for you, they were gentlemen. So now she has to be afraid that every man, who knows what his intentions may be.

THE FIRST ANNIVERSARY

- 2014 -

"

To be torn between celebrating the happy occasion of your daughter's second birthday and helping your wife through one of the hardest days of the year just makes the day impossible.

Chad

Jessi

When you think of anniversaries, most people think of a joyful celebration, but not all anniversaries are worth celebrating. As we entered the fall and the anniversary of the attack approached, I became more withdrawn and anxious. A year ago, I had been joyfully preparing for an Alice in Wonderland birthday party, a woman full of joy and hope, celebrating her daughter's first year of life. This year, I was a woman traumatized, dealing with PTSD and dreading the approach of her own daughter's birthday, the day that would forever mark the darkest moment of my life.

As the anniversary of the attack neared, I became more withdrawn. I dissociated more. I had more flashbacks. To be honest, I didn't want to plan a party. I was still struggling through every day, just barely managing to go to work, spend time with my kids, take care of the house, and do all the little things that make up a life. As the anniversary neared, I didn't even really want to do any of that.

At the same time, I felt terrible about not wanting to plan something special for my daughter's second birthday. The whole day filled me with dread. I couldn't have people over to my house again. I couldn't throw myself into planning a special day with a theme. It was too much. Just thinking about doing any of that made me want to puke. I cried a lot. I was so sad. And I was trying so hard not to show it to my kids. It was my daughter's birthday. She should be happy and excited and the center of attention. It shouldn't be about me. But X had made sure that day would never solely be about my daughter ever again.

Chad and I finally decided to get away from our house entirely for my daughter's birthday. We went to Omaha and had a party at the children's museum there. It was as different from a party at our house as I could make it. I hoped the different setting and a limited guest list that I would be able to enjoy the day. Our group was small, just our family, my parents, Dan and Nancy's family, and my friend Jill and her daughter. We rented a small party room where we had cake and presents then we took the kids around the museum to explore.

But it wasn't enough. The day of my daughter's birth was still the day I had been attacked. Even though I tried to keep my focus on my kids, I remained anxious, looking around and watching for any threat. It felt like someone was watching me. I spent the whole day waiting for something bad to happen.

And I felt like a horrible mother. Who doesn't enjoy their own daughter's birthday? Why couldn't I just have my life back? A year later it still felt like the attack had happened yesterday and was tainting even the good things in my life. And because the prosecutor had refused to press charges, I was never going to get justice. I began to wonder if I would ever be able to move forward or if I was going to be stuck in this horrible state forever.

Chad

As awful as the immediate aftermath of the attack was, the first anniversary was equally as hard. I love my wife and kids more than life itself, and to be torn between celebrating the happy occasion of your daughter's second birthday and helping your wife through one of the hardest days of the year just makes the day impossible.

In the weeks before our daughter's birthday, Jess was distant. You could tell she was trying to hold it together, but she was sad, emotional, angry. It was easy to set her off, and she would often disappear into a non-responsive state.

I don't remember much about the actual party we had in Omaha for our daughter. I was too busy trying to be a happy, excited dad and a supportive husband. The whole day is something of a blur. I do remember the smile on my daughter's face as we went around the children's museum. She was so excited to be the center of attention, to have cake and presents. My son was overflowing with joy, as well. I tried so hard to focus on that, to know that there could still be joy on this day that brought so many negative memories and emotions.

I still do that when the past resurfaces in some way – I try to find the joy.

Susan Barngrover, Ph.D.

(taken from the trial transcript)

Q: And what happens to her on this anniversary date?

A: She becomes more emotional. She becomes more irritable. She becomes more jumpy. Again, what you would expect from that nervous energy. It's unfortunate because it's the anniversary of her daughter's birthday, and so that causes a lot of ambivalence because she would want to be happy, but her body unconsciously remembers and reinvokes those feelings and so she is much more dissociative, more weepy during that time. And that's what you would expect.

Jessi

We made it through the anniversary, but I still felt stuck. I still hungered for justice. And then I had to go back to court because the restraining order was going to expire. We had to go through the entire process again. We once again headed to the Adult Abuse office on November 10, 2014 and sat with a victim advocate who helped us fill out the paperwork.

On November 25, we were standing in the hallway at the court-house waiting for our hearing when I felt this incredible heat on my back, almost as if someone were holding a flame against my spine. Afraid to turn around, I asked Chad to look behind me. He saw X's dad standing just a few feet away staring at me. I don't know if he was sizing me up or trying to intimidate me, but it was uncomfortable either way. Thankfully, X did not show up for the hearing, and the judge granted me a new order of protection.

Every time a sexual assault survivor has to appear in court, it can be traumatizing. And it was no different for me. Even though the hearing was simple, and X didn't contest the order of protection, as soon as the hearing was over, I ran out to our car where I started dry heaving. There seemed to be no end in sight to the trauma I kept reliving.

TIME TO MOVE

- 2015 -

"

This was our dream home. This was
the house we were going to raise
our children, the home where we
could grow old together.

Jessi

Jessi

I continued on through the next couple of months in much the same state. By May 2015, it had been 3 1/2 years since the attack and I was not making progress. I remember one day where I was just staring at my computer screen, realizing I didn't care about anything. I didn't care if Chad came to have coffee with me or whether I got any work done. I wasn't excited to see my kids come home from school. I didn't want to eat. The world felt as if it had been stripped of all color.

I made an emergency appointment with Dr. Barngrover and walked into her office in a sweatshirt – no bra, no make-up, hair a mess. I told her I simply didn't care anymore. I wasn't suicidal, but I didn't feel too far away from that. I told her the world seemed gray. This is the visit where she taught me how to find my "happy place" in my mind, that small beach with turquoise water where I can feel the soft sand under my feet.

Before the attack, my happy place might have been my home. I loved my house. Chad and I had designed and built it and filled it with love and laughter. Until that dreadful night when our house became the scene of my worst nightmare. We had tried so hard to reclaim our home, to be able to live in this place that we had poured so much time and effort into. But every time I went home, every time I went to bed, every time I went to the basement to work, I lived in the space where my attack had taken place.

If you had asked us, we would have told you we didn't want to move. This was our dream home. Chad and I had picked out every fixture, designed every space. This was the house we were going to raise our children, the home where we could grow old together. I wanted to continue to love it. I wanted to live here. But I couldn't. And neither could Chad.

That summer, we started talking about moving. Just short, indirect conversations, neither of us wanting to say that we needed to leave. Finally, one day while we were both in the kitchen, I told Chad, "I feel like we just keep talking around the topic of staying in this house or leaving, neither of us wanting to lay all the cards on the table." That's when Chad finally said what we had both been thinking: "I don't want to live in this house anymore. It is just too big of a reminder of what happened and I want a fresh start for us."

A weight immediately lifted off my shoulders. I felt the same way, but I had been stuck on the idea that I didn't want to let X dictate how we would continue to live our lives. But the reality was our lives had changed. Something terrible had happened in our home, and every day we lived there was a reminder of that night. We were finally ready to admit that our lives were not going to play out exactly as we had dreamed, but we had a choice about what we were going to do next.

Chad

We loved that house. We had dreamed, designed, planned, and built it. When we were building it, we would talk about how the house would grow with us, how we would grow as a family in it. The day we moved in, I could see my kids growing up there, the family gatherings we would have, the laughter and love we would fill it with, but just a few short months later, that vision lay in pieces at my feet. After the attack, I just couldn't picture a future there anymore. I was done with it.

I'm sure it's a great house for someone else now. Maybe they'll fill it with laughter, host family dinners, and watch their kids grow up. But I knew it wouldn't work for our family long before Jess and I reached the decision to move. The memories we made there would never be free of the attack. It would always linger in the background of every happy moment.

You know how in some movies the trauma is so deep the character ends up burning the house down just to feel free? I get it now. It's not really about the fire—it's about letting go. Sometimes staying just traps you in the past. And sometimes, the healthiest thing you can do is walk away and start fresh somewhere else.

Jessi

Now that we had made the decision to move, we had to decide where we wanted to go. We were ready for a fresh start, and we thought that meant not just moving out of our home but making a clean break and starting over in a new city. Several people told us they thought we were running away from our problems, but we were set on getting a clean slate. To the dismay of our parents, we narrowed our options down to Denver or Tampa, even going so far as to schedule a visit to Florida over Labor Day weekend.

We flew in on Friday afternoon and headed for Sarasota and on Saturday we met with a realtor who had secured multiple appointments and showings for us. We fell in love with a community called Lakewood Ranch. It had schools, shopping areas, soccer fields, walking trails, golf courses and pools. I started tearing up as we toured the community and told Chad I thought it was a sign that this was where we were meant to be. We met with several builders while we were there, and we knew that this was the place for us.

We visited a few more communities on Sunday, but nothing felt like home the way Lakewood Ranch did. We returned home on Monday and shared the floor plan and the community's marketing materials with our parents. We contacted a realtor who provided comps on our house and made a recommendation on a price for our house. We agreed, and within a day he had a photographer taking photos of our house and a sign in our front yard. We were excited to move forward with our new life in Florida.

While we waited for our house to sell, the realtor in Florida was pressuring us to put down a deposit on one of the lots, but we remained hesitant because we weren't seeing any movement on our house. We decided to wait a little bit longer before making the deposit. As excited as we were to move on with our lives, we didn't want to put ourselves in a tough financial position. In addition, the second anniversary of the attack was approaching and once again pulling our focus into the past.

Jessi

While we had been frustrated by the slow sale of our house, we quickly learned that the wait had a purpose. Just a few weeks before the second anniversary of the attack, Chad's mom, Julie, went to the emergency room for what we thought was a urinary tract infection, but it was much more serious than that. She had a kidney infection that had turned septic and the doctors were giving her 24 hours to live. Chad and I rushed to the emergency room where we were required to suit up in plastic gowns and gloves before we could see her.

After visiting for a few minutes, Chad, his dad, and I stepped into a small conference room to share our disbelief and share our grief. How could such a terrible thing be happening at the same time of year? We talked about the things we needed to do, especially calling family and close friends so that those who wanted to could have time with Julie. I wanted to help and volunteered to make the calls. Two of the people at the top of the list were Julie's brother and his wife. X's in-laws.

Chad and his dad both offered to make the call, but I knew that this was something I needed to do. For two years, I had held onto my anger at these two people because they continued to let a monster in their home and to be around their grandchildren. As terrible as the news I had to share was, I hoped that in some way, this call would be a healing moment for me. I grabbed Julie's phone and made the call with sweaty hands. My whole body was shaking, and I worried that I wouldn't be able to get any words out over the lump in my throat.

"Hello?" I said.

"Yes?" she answered.

"I'm calling to let you know that Julie is in the hospital and the doctors have given her 24 hours to live," I told her. "We are trying to notify as many people as possible in case there are people that want to see her."

"I know," she said. "Liz called me." Liz is Chad's sister.

I asked her if she would contact a few other people on our list that I hadn't been able to reach, and when she agreed, I hung up without saying goodbye.

I wish I could say talking to her was some kind of healing moment for me, but it wasn't. I don't know what I expected from the call, but when I hung up I still felt angry and like I wanted to throw up. I don't think I expected her to address the rape directly, but I had hoped I would hear something in her voice – sadness, sympathy, some kind of emotion. She had never been the most approachable person, but I thought surely when she heard my voice on the phone that there might be some sign of remorse or sadness. I would realize months later that Chad's aunt attached no meaning to me one way or the other. As an emotionally driven person, it is hard for me to relate to people on the opposite end of the spectrum. It made me wonder if she had become numb to this type of thing, that perhaps X had displayed other poor behavior in the past and this was her way of coping. I'll never know if that is true, but it is where my thoughts went in the months after the call.

After recovering from the call, our focus returned to Julie who simply refused to go along with the doctors' prognosis. She started to get better, eventually getting off the ventilator and sitting up and eating. After more than two months, she left the hospital and rehab. She still had healing to do, but she was alive.

In the midst of all of this, we finally received an offer on our house. We were pleased with the offer, but the scare with Julie was making us rethink our decision to move away from our families. When Chad and I sat down to talk about it, it became apparent that we were trying to force the move to Florida to work. The higher cost of building a home in Florida would mean a change to our standard of living, and being in Florida would mean that we would not be close by if Julie's health took a turn for the worse. We tried to rationalize both those things by telling each other if we lived in Florida, we wouldn't need to take big vacations and that Florida was only a short plane ride away if we needed to get back quickly. But in the end, we realized we were trying to talk ourselves into a move that we should have been excited about. After talking through what seemed like hundreds of scenarios, we decided to postpone our move to Florida. However, we did still want to get out of the house that continued to remind us of the worst day of our lives, so we accepted the offer and told our families that we were staying put.

When we told my parents, they were thrilled, and to be honest, that hurt a little bit. Chad and I were really sad, and I was really, really sad. I knew that staying in Kansas City was the right thing to do financially and so our young children could be close to their grandparents, but I really felt like I was in mourning for the life I could have had. I could picture us there in our house, our neighborhood, and our new life. Even now, we still follow the Florida builder on Facebook and look at homes in the area. That dream still lives on even if it isn't the dream we can pursue right now.

We now needed a place to live and began looking the same day we accepted the offer, rushing to find a realtor who would work to find us a new home before our buyers needed us to get out. We found a beautiful new home that was nearly ready to move into that was in the same subdivision as some of our close friends, Bob and Ashley. When we asked the new buyers of our house if they would let us rent it back from them until our house was ready, they asked if we would pay the rent in the form of furniture, including our bedroom set. That request was a gift from God. We would be able to move into our new home without any tangible reminders of the rape. It finally felt like we were on the road to healing.

Jessi

Despite the new start in a new home, I still struggled with the loss of any opportunity to hold X accountable for what he had done. Without justice, how could I truly move on? And how could I move on knowing there was no public record of what X had done, no way to keep others safe? These thoughts weighed heavily on me as we passed the second anniversary, and I decided not to pursue a renewal of the restraining order. The more time passes without any contact with an attacker, the harder it becomes to obtain a restraining order. I didn't want to go through that process again with less chance for success. What I did want, though, was some kind of justice for everything that had happened to me.

My friend Ashley began urging me to talk with her dad, Paul, who was a civil lawyer. She thought he might be able to help once he heard our story. I was skeptical that there was anything that Paul could do for us, but I was desperate for even a whiff of justice, so we agreed to meet with him. We knew Paul in passing, having met him at birthday parties for Ashley's kids and other functions, but this was different.

At our first meeting, Paul asked us to tell him our story. He took notes and asked us to elaborate on certain events. As I spoke, my words were often inaudible, my voice cracking with choked back tears and sadness. I stared at my hands, my fingers nervously picking at each other. When I had gotten through the worst of the retelling, I looked up to see Paul looking back with tears in his eyes. I felt seen and heard and knew that I could trust Paul to handle my story with care, so I wasn't prepared for what he said next.

He carefully placed his yellow legal pad and pen on the table, then leaned back in his chair, interlocking his fingers with his elbows on the arms of the chair and proceeded to bring up the one word I never wanted to hear again – intent. He told us we could sue X under the pretext of intent or negligence. I shuddered when he said the word. After all of this, it was going to come down to the same thing that had derailed the criminal case – proving what was going on inside of X's head at the moment of the attack. Noting my reaction, Paul hurried to reassure us that the definition of intent in civil court is different from the definition in criminal court.

In the criminal sense, a prosecutor must prove beyond a reasonable doubt that X knew what he was doing and intentionally came into our bedroom to commit the act. In the civil sense, the attorney must prove what was going on in his mind when he committed the act. Civil attorneys still have a difficult task in proving intent, but the level at which they present the convincing evidence is much lower.

Paul also told us that in civil court, no one is found guilty or not guilty. The only determination would be whether X would be held liable for damages, which would come in the form of monetary compensation. I couldn't wrap my head around the idea of collecting money for what had happened to me. I didn't want to be paid off. I wanted my attacker in jail. Even if the judge found in our favor, X would still be walking free, carrying on his life as if nothing had happened. I wasn't sure what a civil judgment would do for me. Would that even come close to satisfying my need for justice?

Paul offered to represent us if we decided to pursue the civil route, but he truthfully told us that it would still be a long, hard road. If the case made it to trial without a settlement being reached beforehand, we would be forced to relive the events of the day many more times. When we left his office, we had a lot to think about.

Chad

When we went to our meeting with Paul, I walked in just wanting what was best for Jess, but as soon as we met Paul, I felt an unexpected sense of calm. This felt right, like we were finally where we needed to be.

Paul was honest about our chances of winning and very direct, but both Jess and I could feel his compassion. The odds were a little long for everything to go in our favor, but I didn't care. If this was what Jess needed to do, then I was going to stand beside her.

Plenty of people told us to let it go and stop looking back, but we felt strongly that we needed to see this through. We weren't chasing a particular outcome. In fact, it took Jess a while to come to terms with the idea of asking for money. This just felt like the right thing to do – to stand up and follow every legal path available to us to hold X accountable, no matter where it led.

PURSUING A CIVIL SUIT

"

It had been almost two years since the rape, and it seemed like a lot of people we knew didn't understand why we were still "hung up" on it.

Chad

Jessi

We spent the car ride home from Paul's office carefully sorting through the facts. Both Chad and I finally felt like we were making progress in moving on past the attack. Going to trial would dredge up all the details and bring back all the emotions. It would also expose us and our family to scrutiny and could potentially cost us a lot of money. And for what? What was our ultimate goal if we couldn't prevent X from doing this to another person.

As we talked our options over, it finally came down to one thing: we wanted to hold X accountable in whatever way we could. If we got a judgment holding X liable for the attack, it would be a public record that would be tied to X's name forever. Every time he tried to get a job or buy a house or a car, it would come up. Future employers could find it in a public search of court records. While it wasn't the same as a criminal conviction, it would at least make others aware of what had happened. We decided that if we didn't at least try, we would always feel like we had left something undone, that we would always carry around a void that needed to be filled.

On October 27, 2015, Paul filed a petition for damages with the Jackson County Circuit Court. On November 5, X was served with papers officially notifying him of the pending case, and our case was assigned to Judge Sandra Midkiff.

Chad

Deciding to pursue a civil verdict wasn't easy, and even after we made the decision, a lot of people questioned if we were doing the right thing. It had been almost two years since the rape, and it seemed like a lot of people we knew didn't understand why we were still "hung up" on it. Until you've been through it, you have no idea how something like this will completely alter your life.

People would say stuff that was definitely not helpful.

"Just get over it."

"It's time to move on."

"Why do you guys want to go through the civil trial? Why do you want to put yourselves through all that?"

People would ask you why, but they wouldn't wait for an answer. It was more like a statement. They weren't asking me to share with them. They weren't asking and pausing, waiting for me to answer. They were essentially trying to tell me what they thought I should do.

Susan Barngrover, Ph.D.

I talked the decision to pursue a civil case over with my therapist. During the trial, our attorney asked her to explain why it was so important to me. – Jessi
(taken from the trial transcript)

Q: And we've talked about the fact that you encouraged her to seek a legal remedy. What role does justice have in trying to help treat a patient like Jessi Bixler?

A. From my experience when a woman sees that there has been a legal remedy, at least our culture has not let her down. This man let her down by violating her trust, but the legal remedy says that we as a society care about what happened to her and we care about women, and it helps the woman feel less powerless that there has been a remedy. Also Jessi is very concerned that other women will be hurt and she wants to make sure that this is a deterrent so that other women are not hurt.

Jessi

After making the decision to file the civil suit, we got through the second anniversary. It felt like we were actually taking steps to get our lives back on track. I was enjoying my new job and was resolved to pursue the civil case. It seemed like maybe our lives were taking a turn for the better.

Then on a Friday morning in early December, the human resources director at my company called and told me that they were eliminating my position. I was dumbfounded. I knew that they had been making cuts throughout the company, but we were only two weeks away from launching the new website, a project they had specifically hired me to lead. Unsure what the future held, I began to call the vendors who had been working with me on the project to let them know I would no longer be their contact person. Most wished me the best, asked about getting paid (something I could no longer help them with), and took the name of the new contact, but one call was different.

I spoke directly with the owner of the company and after expressing his shock, his attitude quickly changed to one of excitement. He told me, "We've always talked about how if you became available how we'd love to have you as part of the team, but because you were our client, we could never say anything." I was flattered but still completely overwhelmed by the enormity of unexpectedly losing my job. I thanked him for his interest, passed on the information of the new contact person for the website and hung up, unsure if anything would come of our short interaction. The owner was persistent. Texting me multiple times over the weekend and asking me to come in and spend "a day in the life" with the company. I agreed and spent the following Tuesday checking it out. At the end of the day, he offered me the job, and I accepted.

Not long after starting with my new company, one of the representatives of the partners we worked with was scheduled to spend the morning with us going over prospective customers. One of the companies was based in Columbia, Missouri. When I heard that, my stomach dropped, and I became nauseous. X and his wife both worked for an insurance company in Columbia, and even though I logically knew that the odds of running into either of them was small in a company the size of the insurance company and a city the size of Columbia, it didn't matter. I couldn't even stop in Columbia for a bathroom break on a car trip because of my fear of seeing them. There was no way I could manage to go there for a work trip.

I finally decided to give one of the owners of my company a brief description of what had happened to me and explain that there was no way I could participate in this project. I had no idea how he would respond, but he immediately promised that no one at the company would do business with that company in any way. He told me that the employees of his company were more important than "dirty business." After all I had endured, I can't express how validating it was for someone to believe me and put my feelings above the potential for new business.

Jessi

The second half of 2015 took a lot of twists and turns – Chad's mom's illness, my new job and getting let go from that job, our decision not to move to Florida, and deciding to file the civil case – and our lives were now heading in a new direction. In some ways it felt a little bit like the fresh start we had been looking for with our planned move to Florida. I had worked through a lot of the initial trauma surrounding the rape and could now start delving into some other areas, including my relationships with family and friends.

I started with my mom who began sharing some of her feelings with me. I was finally in a place to listen to someone else's experience and be able to engage with them about it. I felt like my mom and I had made real progress in our relationship. One of the things I had asked everyone was not to tell other people until I was ready, and I was finally there. I told my mom she could tell her two best friends, but I was not prepared for what she said next: "Well, I already told them. I just felt so alone and needed someone to talk to, and we tell each other everything."

I didn't know what to say. I was crushed. I felt betrayed. I had lost control of my own story. I didn't say anything to my mom, but I did bring it up the next time I met with Dr. Barngrover. She encouraged me to simply explain to my mom how it made me feel and why it made me feel that way.

Not long after, I did talk with my mom who felt terrible that she had hurt me and broken my trust. We both agreed that we needed to communicate better in the future. I felt like that discussion was a healing moment, a time when I got to reclaim my story and speak up for myself. It wasn't until I was writing this book that I would learn my mom felt differently.

Mom/Debbie

I vividly remember that discussion. I probably felt a little different than Jess. I didn't intend for it to be that kind of conversation. It's part of why I've been afraid to say anything since because I just didn't like that day in that conversation then. So, I've been really careful to not say anything because I didn't want that to happen again.

After that, I felt even a little bit more nervous about things that I would say around Jess because I was afraid that we would have a similar kind of blow up. I obviously never intended to hurt Jess, but it did. And that day I was just scared to say anything because I'm afraid of a blow up like that. It was not a comfortable day. It wasn't good. I felt terrible. I know that something I said caused it, but when I said it, I had no idea that it would trigger the response. That's what's made me scared and nervous about what to say in the future. How do I know what I can say and when?

Jessi

I haven't talked much about my brother because at the time of the attack, we weren't close. Not because anything bad had happened, but we were just at very different places in our lives, him living the bachelor life and me working and raising a young family. I knew it was up to me to reach out to Josh, so I invited him to Karma Koffee in Omaha, Nebraska, a coffee shop my aunt and uncle had introduced us to. One of the owners had also been raped and now worked alongside a local hospital to improve the rooms where rape kits are conducted.

After some small talk, I told Josh I wanted to give him the opportunity to ask me any questions he had. Most of his information about the attack had come from my dad who had gotten the info from my mom. One of his first questions was: "Why didn't Chad or Dad kill him right there or at least beat the shit out of him?" My brother had been carrying around a load of anger toward Chad and my dad since the attack, some of it probably rooted in his own rage that he wasn't there to protect me.

We both started to cry. I was so thankful that he was sharing his feelings with me. I told him that I loved him and that he couldn't stay angry with Chad and Dad. If I had learned one thing in this horrible situation, I had learned that you can't predict how you'll react when faced with your worst fears. Adrenaline and shock create different responses in each person that makes it impossible to know how you would or wouldn't respond to a terrifying event. I told my brother that right after the attack both Chad and Dad's brains were struggling to process what had happened. I also shared with him that it was probably a good thing that neither had done anything because I had needed Dad to drive me to the hospital, and I didn't need Chad to be sitting in a jail cell for murder. I needed him right beside me.

That conversation marked a change in my relationship with my brother. As time passed, we would talk more frequently and become closer. Today, he is both my brother, my friend, and one of my biggest cheerleaders.

Josh

When Jess asked me to go to coffee, I was terrified. I didn't want to hear what she had to say, but I did want to hear. I had a lot of questions; I wanted to know specifics. I'm the type of person who has to map things out and see step by step how things happened because it was hard for me to understand. I certainly wasn't looking forward to the conversation, but at the same time, it probably needed to have happened even sooner.

After we talked, I immediately felt closer to Jess and like I could understand more, but I didn't feel good because for me, it was kind of like it had just happened. I got more specifics and now I could visualize how it happened because she was very descriptive, which was what I needed. But I still needed to process all of it.

Jessi

My dad was the only person I hadn't talked to, so the next time they were in town for a visit, I invited my dad out for dinner and some beers on a Friday night. I didn't tell him what I wanted to talk about until after we had ordered. I invited him to share what was on his mind. He told me how angry he still was and how he kept replaying what happened and wondering why he hadn't done more.

For my part of the conversation, I talked with him about how upset I was with my mom for telling her friends without my permission, which opened the door for him to talk about how he was also hurt because he felt like she talked with her friends more than she talked to him. I think he really wanted someone to talk to. I encouraged him to talk to her and even broach the conversation, which was really outside his comfort zone.

We ended the evening on some lighter topics and a big hug. I know I felt a lot lighter than when we had walked in.

Dad/Tony

The night Jess wanted to go out for beers was fabulous. It was nice to know that I was getting her back. I didn't want to be part of the males that she couldn't be around. She's such a strong woman. That's all I can say. I just don't know how to put it because I don't know too damn many people that could go through that and do like she's done and be able to talk about it.

I don't remember what we talked about that night. I was just so ecstatic to be with her that I couldn't really tell you. It was just father, daughter time. I knew we were going to be all right. That trauma that she had, it took time away from us and it was hard on her that just to be able to have her smile and be happy was just fantastic. We just talked like we normally did. It was great to have that time back, and I was very thankful for that.

FINDING FAITH

- 2016 -

"

A lot of the heaviness I had been carrying, the feeling that everyone would judge if they knew my story, lifted because of the beautiful response of the people we told in our faith community.

Jessi

Jessi

.

Up to this point in my life, I wouldn't describe myself as particularly religious. I had grown up Catholic, but Chad and I didn't regularly attend any church. Honestly, after the attack, if I thought too much about God, my main question was "Why would you let this happen to me?" But in January, my grandpa died, and our kids started asking questions about death, God, and prayer that I didn't really have great answers to. We started talking about going to church as if it were another thing to check off our parenting list. You know, "Our kids are getting older and asking questions, so we need to give them some kind of faith foundation."

With our own faith being pretty much non-existent, we were open to suggestions about churches from other people. Our son's friend's dad had asked a couple of times if we wanted to attend with them, but we weren't quite ready. Finally, in February 2016, we walked through the doors of Eagle Creek Church for the first time. It was like walking into a foreign country. The preacher wore jeans. They sang songs with a rock beat. There were no pictures of Jesus on the walls. Everything I knew about church didn't apply here. I just wanted to keep my head down and blend into the background, so I could decide for myself whether this was something I wanted.

Thankfully, that was not to be. We ran into our son's friend's dad, Bo, who became our tour guide to church. He showed us where to check in our kids, where to find the coffee and led us to the main auditorium where the music was loud, the lights were bright, and the fog machines were on full blast. I looked at Chad with a questioning glance to make sure we hadn't mistakenly walked into a rock concert. After four songs, the pastor stepped onto the stage, welcomed everyone, made announcements and launched into his sermon. It was a high-energy, casual service far removed from the staid, liturgical services of my Catholic youth. I enjoyed it, but I wasn't really sure it was the right place for our family.

Despite my uncertainty, we returned the next week, feeling a little more confident since we at least knew where to drop our kids off and how to find the coffee. The band launched into their first song, and by the end of it, I had tears streaming down my face. Some of the weight I had been carrying was gone and a piece of my soul was being healed. I don't have a big conversion story, just the knowledge that despite everything that had happened to me, there was a God in heaven who loved me and wanted good things for me. That knowledge would change my life and become a part of my healing journey.

We continued to attend church regularly, and after a couple of months, the pastor asked for people to host a community group where several families would get together in our homes and study the Bible together. Chad and I both felt like it was time for us to raise our hands to volunteer. Our friendships and even our relationships with our families had changed so much with the attack, with some falling to the side. We needed a new community.

We started with three other couples. Two of those couples are still in our group so many years later, and one of the women is now my best friend. Everyone in our circle before this we had known before the attack.

It's hard to put into words what surviving a sexual assault does to your relationships. Some get stronger, some die, and some just stagnate. As the survivor, you always kind of wonder what labels other people are putting on you in their heads. Are they busy comparing the person you were before to the person you are now? Did they like the before-attack you better than the present you? And whether others are pressuring you or not, there's always a little thought in the back of your mind telling you that you should try harder to be more like the person you were before the worst happened even if that's not who you even want to be now.

Then there's the pity. You never really know who is looking at you with genuine sorrow for what you've gone through and wants to help you pick up the pieces because they love you and want you to heal in whatever form that takes and who is just thinking about you like, "Poor Jessi. How will she ever recover?" Some of these thoughts may not be fair to other people who just want to help, but as you try to put the pieces of your life back together, relationships can be the trickiest part to manage

In a lot of ways, it was refreshing to meet new people, people who didn't know me before. I could simply be the person I was right then with no comparison to the before. If people were going to want to be my friend, they would want to be the friend of the person I was right then. But in other ways, opening up our home and our lives to others was scary, especially with the undercurrent of religion a strong thread holding us together. I didn't know if these new people would judge me as unworthy because of what happened to me.

But the people in our community group are loving, open people. When we told them what had happened to me, it was really the first time I had told anyone outside of close friends and family other than the people I had told when it affected my job. It turned out to be one of the best experiences. I didn't feel any judgment or shame or anything like that, and because of that, I would later be bold enough and brave enough to start sharing my story with strangers. A lot of the heaviness I had been carrying, the feeling that everyone would judge if they knew my story, lifted because of the beautiful response of the people we told in our faith community.

Jessi

While we were learning about faith and what it meant to be part of a community that accepted us as the broken people we were, preparations for the civil trial were ongoing. Now, well into our third year after the rape, I finally felt like we were taking some steps toward holding X accountable for what he did to me – and those around me. But the process was hard, and a lot of days, I could barely hold it together.

In February 2016, just over three years after the assault, the court held the first meeting related to our case. At the case management meeting, the judge set the trial date for March 27, 2017, more than a year away. For the next 13 months, I would not only have to relive the events of the attack but the trauma as well. The year would be long, exhausting, hurtful, and difficult to survive, but Chad and I were still in agreement that this was the right thing to do.

Our lawyer, Paul, submitted the Petition of Damages, which officially notified the court of our four claims:

- **Negligence:** X breached a duty of care through careless or reckless conduct that caused us harm.
- **Battery:** Intentional, unwanted, harmful, or offensive touching of another person and the most direct civil claim

against X for the physical contact of the assault. It squarely frames the assault as an intentional act.

- **Loss of Consortium:** Because Chad and I were filing the suit together, it spoke to the loss of companionship, intimacy, support, and affection because of the injury to me.
- **Punitive Damages:** These were meant to punish X directly for outrageous conduct and deter others from similar acts. Rape is an intentional, violent act that courts often find warrants punishment beyond compensatory damages.

Paul wanted us to file all four claims together to cover both intentional and negligent theories of the crime. It also maximized potential damages and created multiple paths to liability, so even if the court dismissed one of the claims, the others would still stand.

In a criminal trial, the person charged with the crime will assert their guilt or innocence during a court proceeding where they enter a plea. In civil court, that process occurs on paper only in a document called Answer to the Pleadings where the defendant goes through the Petition for Damages that contains the counts against them and admits or denies the assertions in each paragraph. Other than agreeing to the basic facts of who we were, where we lived, and the time of the party, X denied everything. "In further answer and defense, Defendant denies each and every allegation of Count (#) of Plaintiffs' Petition not specifically admitted herein," read the Answer to Pleadings. Over and over I read those words until I was sick of them.

In my head, I knew X wouldn't admit to any wrongdoing, but seeing his denial of what he had done to me in black and white was still disturbing. This man had ruined my life, and now he was going to act like he had done nothing at all? Seeing his denial in writing made me all the more determined to pursue the civil suit.

Jessi

When we initially chose to bring a civil case, our end goal was to get our day in court, but just as a lot of criminal cases end in a plea deal, so, too, do most civil cases end in a settlement. Paul wanted us to submit a settlement request to see if we could save everyone some time, money, and emotional stress. Taking the settlement route would offer multiple benefits, even if we didn't settle:

- We could get our judgment and not have to go through the agony of a trial.
- It would test whether X was willing to resolve things quickly without dragging everyone through the year-long process of depositions, hearings, and a trial.
- Our costs would be lower.
- It would set the tone for what Paul thought the case was worth.
- It showed we were prepared to go to court if needed, but that we were also open to an alternative resolution,
- It would force X (or his insurance) to think about the risk and potential damages of settling the case in court.
- It was a process we would probably have to go through anyway as many courts encourage, and sometimes require,

attorneys to engage in settlement talks before going to trial.

I honestly wasn't sure how I felt about settling. I wanted X to be held accountable. I wanted the world to know what he had done to me. I wanted his crime attached to his name, forever a warning to everyone else. I didn't know if settling was the right thing to do, but I did know that I wanted no part of any settlement that would hide what he had done.

On February 26, 2016, Paul sent a certified letter to X's lawyers requesting a payment settlement with a deadline of March 1. At their request, Paul extended the deadline to March 15 at 5 p.m. On March 15, X's insurance company withdrew its reservation of rights, which meant the company was waiving any legal rights or defense they would have had not to cover X in this case. Essentially, that meant the insurance company was agreeing X's "alleged" acts were covered by his insurance policy.

It is an interesting aspect of insurance law that an act like rape could be covered by insurance if you are sued for damages. X's attorneys would claim that he was too drunk to know that he wasn't in his own bedroom and didn't recognize that I was not his wife when the attack occurred. This meant his actions could be covered under the area of "negligence" on his insurance policy. As unbelievable as this was and still is to me, it is the way insurance works in situations like this. Essentially, we were suing X, but his insurance company would pay any damages if they were awarded. That also meant we were negotiating a settlement with the insurance company – not directly with X.

March 15 arrived with no response from X's lawyers. As the 5 p.m. deadline approached, X's lawyer finally reached out to Paul at 4:35 p.m. – asking for another extension. X's attorneys said they wanted my and Chad's depositions and the insurance company's lawyer's evaluation of the case. Paul denied the request, which made our settlement request null and void. Paul felt X's lawyers had enough information in the police reports and access to X and his story of what had happened, and he pointed out to X's lawyer that he felt a jury verdict in this case would exceed the limits of X's insurance policy.

We had barely started the civil litigation process, and we were already discouraged, angry, and confused. I felt like the insurance company was playing games. They could have asked for any of the information they wanted long before March 15. Even Paul was shocked by X's attorney's response to our request for settlement talks. Once again, we had done everything the legal system required of us, and it felt like once again, the justice system was letting us down. With no prior experience dealing with litigation, and despite Paul's best attempts to prepare us, we simply hadn't known what to expect. It seemed this process would be longer and harder than we had anticipated, but despite our discouragement, we knew we wanted to press on. We had a trial to prepare for.

Chad

With settlement off the table, we moved into the discovery phase of trial preparation where evidence is gathered and shared between the parties involved. This included depositions. A deposition is a formal, recorded interview where a witness or party to the case answers questions under oath. Depositions gather facts and testimony before a trial, give attorneys an idea of how witnesses will perform on the stand, preserve testimony in case a witness can't appear at trial, and pin down a person's story so they can't easily change it later without being challenged.

X's deposition was first on the calendar on May 5, 2016. Paul had asked me to attend, and I agreed. Jess stayed home. She wasn't ready to see X or be in the same room with him. It was a good choice for her because as I stepped off the elevator, the first person I saw was X's dad. I knew then that it could be a long day. Paul immediately stepped in and took me into the men's bathroom to have a private conversation about how the day would go. He told me it could take a few hours and be extremely difficult to listen to.

I had prepared myself to hear terrible things from X. I was ready for the worst. What I wasn't prepared for was how difficult it was just to hear Paul ask the questions. The worst day of my life was reduced to a simple litany of fact-based questions, none of which conveyed the enormity of the tsunami that had hit my family. I think maybe it was a blessing that X chose to "plead the fifth" to every question, refusing to answer on the ground that he might incriminate himself, so I didn't have to sit through his answers.

Paul told us afterward that he wasn't surprised that X exercised his fifth amendment right. He said X's attorney probably told him to do that, so X would not be held in contempt for failing to testify. However, we also learned that pleading the fifth in a civil trial is different than doing so in a criminal one. In a criminal trial, when someone invokes the fifth amendment to avoid answering a question, judges and juries are not allowed to attach any negative connotation to it. It can not be viewed as an admission of guilt. In a civil trial, however, the fifth amendment does not prohibit the judge or jury from attaching a negative connotation to that decision, meaning a judge or jury would be allowed to infer guilt from a defendant's choice to invoke the fifth amendment.

With X refusing to answer any questions, the deposition was over quickly. Twenty minutes after sitting down at the table, I walked out the door to meet Jess at a coffee shop. We talked about the deposition, but I only gave her a broad overview of what happened, avoiding details because I wasn't sure how she would handle it. I don't really remember what I said to her, but I vividly remember the emotions – doubt, fear, worry over whether this was the right choice or if I was simply doing something that would further hurt our family.

Jessi

Our depositions were up next. They would take place at
Paul's office but would be conducted by the insurance-ap-
pointed attorney. Paul did a great job preparing us for what would
take place. He told me he did not think the other lawyer would be
rude or offensive; in fact, he expected the attorney to be sympathetic. However, he also warned us not to consider him a friend. As
he went over the logistics of how a deposition works, Paul also told
us X had the right to be present if he chose to be.

My heart dropped. I panicked just thinking about X sitting
there, watching me as I answered questions about what he had done
to me. I couldn't fathom how I would manage to hold it together
if he were allowed to sit in the same room with me. On July 20,
the day of the deposition, I could barely force myself to walk off
the elevator and down the hall, fearing that every step was taking
me closer to my attacker. My steps were stilted and robotic, like
the Tin Man from the Wizard of Oz. I pushed open the door to the
room and relaxed slightly when there was no sign of X. My limbs
loosened slightly and breathing became easier. This day would still
be awful, but at least facing my attacker was not on the agenda.

The attorney introduced himself, and we got started reliving
the worst night of my life. Paul had been right. As X's attorney

worked his way from the easy questions about who I was and where I worked to the attack itself, my anxiety continued to rise. I often answered questions with a simple yes or no, each question bringing me closer to the event that changed my life forever. I made it through recounting the attack but needed to take a break when we got to questions about what happened next. Sobbing, I practically ran back to Paul's office where Chad pulled me into his arms and held me. For 10 minutes, I worked to collect myself, to put those emotions in a place where I could wall them off enough to finish my testimony. When Paul came in, I was ready to finish.

The attorney continued to walk me through the events of that night and the aftermath. So many of the questions were things I could not answer, specific details that my traumatized brain simply could not remember. It was clear from the tenor of the questions that X's attorney was going to try to paint what happened to me as a mistake. X got drunk and entered the wrong bedroom, thinking I was his wife. I didn't believe that scenario then, and I don't believe it now. I just hoped a judge wouldn't believe it either.

When the attorney asked me for examples of how the attack had negatively affected my life, it was hard to come up with just one. The life I had known before was gone, vanished in those wee morning hours of Dec. 1. I took one stab at describing it for the attorney in my last answer of the day:

"It's affected every part of my life. I'm not the person that I was before. I'm scared all the time. I jump whenever I hear somebody who has the same first name. I jump every time I see a white truck. I couldn't go in the basement of our home for months. I couldn't be alone in our house for months. I couldn't be around men by myself. I panicked anytime Chad's not around. Anytime I talk about it, I feel like my throat is closing. I'm angry and depressed. And it's a constant struggle, constantly just have to fight to just get through the day."

Chad

Watching Jess give her deposition was difficult. Not only did she have to walk step by step through the night that haunts her dreams, she also had to give voice to all the things that night had cost her. And then it was my turn.

My deposition focused mainly on what I remembered from that night. Other than a few questions about the early evening, the attorney mostly focused on questions about how many drinks I, X, and Jess had had that night. He also asked me about what happened when Jess came out of the bedroom. His final questions were about the things we had lost, specifically how things had changed in our relationship. I'm not generally a fearful person, but when I look at my response to X's attorney's questions, I am struck by how fear even now still plays an outsized role in our lives.

> "There's always that... fear there when... there's groups. Just don't know what's going to trigger. And just always watching and making sure she's okay, and... she doesn't have a bad experience. You know, as intimacy goes, I guess the number one thing is the spontaneity... There's no spontaneity... [S]ometimes... we'll have to stop, and sometimes she'll cry, and sometimes there are things like

that, and of a fear of hurting her more. Just the little things of, you know, giving my wife a hug and just reaching out and touching someone."

Jessi

Even though we were moving forward with our trial preparation, Paul invited us to his office to discuss our next steps. He wanted to make sure we understood all the possible outcomes of a trial.

We could go to trial, and a jury could order damages in our favor. They could be as low as X's insurance policy limit or they could be exponentially higher. On the other hand, we could go to trial and lose. If the jury sided with X, we would receive nothing. The third option was to try to settle out of court for an amount of damages deemed fair for X and his insurance company.

We still thought a settlement was possible. The thought of having to go through the grueling process of giving my testimony in court was not appealing. In that meeting, Paul prepared us for what a trial could look like. He and his team gave us a two-page list of objections that a jury would contemplate in our case. Things like "If it were me, I would have woken up when he climbed in the bed," "I would have woken up when he took off my underwear," or "I wouldn't have had alcohol at a 1-year-old's birthday party."

That list of questions was devastating. Unlike many rape survivors, up to that point, I had never had anyone question the truth of what happened before. No one had tried to lay the blame for the attack at my door, but now a group of strangers would weigh my words and decide whether to believe me. I began to curl in on myself. It felt as if I were cowering, covering my face, trying to protect myself from an assault on my mental state.

After looking at the options, we chose to pursue settlement because our end goal was simply to attach X's crime to his name.

On August 4, 2016, Paul sent a request for potential settlement to X's and his insurance's attorneys stating our interest in pursuing a settlement with the stipulation that any judgment against X would not include confidentiality, meaning any judgment against X would be publicly accessible, and I would not be restricted from talking about what had happened. X's attorney also was ready to settle and encouraged the insurance company to pay the policy limit. He sent a letter to X's insurance that said, "Considering the history of this case, there is absolutely no question that [the insurance company] acted in bad faith and has failed to protect the defendant's interest."

X's lawyers wanted to settle and didn't understand why the insurance company had passed up the chance to do so in March, sending a letter that stated, "Frankly, I am at a loss why [the insurance company] refused to agree to the policy limit by the March 15, 2016 deadline. [The insurance company] had all of the information necessary to evaluate the claim and conclude that a jury would render a verdict well in excess of [the policy's payout] plus a significant punitive damage verdict."

But the insurance company was still in no mood to settle. They rejected our request on August 31, 2016. At this point, Paul felt the insurance company was acting in bad faith, trying to drag the process out. In his letter to the insurance company, he said, "There was never any secret about what happened. There was never any doubt about the nature and extent of the injury before our clients' depositions and discovery responses. There was never any doubt about the type of people that Chad and Jessi Bixler were before they gave their depositions. In fact, I note that [the insurance company] did not even take their depositions by videotape if their appearance was important. No doubt this is because they knew from their insured the character of Chad and Jessi Bixler."

People sometimes ask us if we ever regretted not extending the deadline. The answer is no. The insurance company seemed to be toying with us, and we had no interest in being their playthings. Declining to extend the deadline gave us some sense of control of the process. But even though we were frustrated and appalled by the insurance company's behavior, we still would have liked to avoid a full-blown trial, so we decided to make one last-ditch effort at a settlement through mediation.

MEDIATIONS

- 2017 -

"

I was so angry that the insurance company was using tactics that played on Jess's trauma.

Chad

Jessi

Mediation is a structured negotiation process where the people on both sides of the dispute try to reach a voluntary settlement with the help of a mediator, who is a neutral third party. Before agreeing to mediation, Paul had sought assurances from the insurance company's attorney that the insurance company was open to negotiating above the stated policy limits.

Throughout the entire civil process, I continued to struggle with the idea of suing X and his insurance company for a large sum of money. I didn't pursue a civil case because I wanted money. I pursued it because it was the only avenue left for me to receive some kind of justice. If the insurance company had agreed to work with us when we first suggested a settlement, we would have been happy to accept the public judgment and a sum of money within the policy limits. Now, however, we felt like the insurance company had been playing games with us, trying to see how far we were willing to take the case. And I was done. I was mad. This awful thing had happened to me, and X and his insurance company were making it as difficult as possible for me to get any kind of justice for an event that had all but destroyed me. At this point, I just wanted them all to pay, so we decided to negotiate over the policy limits.

When the insurance company's lawyer replied that they would negotiate over the policy limits, Paul submitted a request for mediation on November 30, 2016. Ironically, this was exactly three years since the attack and while we were celebrating our daughter's 4th birthday. The party that year was not at our home. We paid for the party package at the indoor pool at a nearby community center and spent the morning hosting a Little Mermaid-themed birthday party for our daughter.

By this point, I was tired of the process, tired of the constant back and forth, tired of the insurance company saying one thing and doing another. I asked Paul if we had to do mediation or if we could just wait for the trial. Paul explained that it would not be a smart decision not to participate in the mediation. He thought there was a good chance that we could resolve things and not have to go through the trauma of a trial. He promised me that even though all parties were required to be at the mediation, X would be kept in a separate conference room on the opposite side of the office from me.

Two months after the mediation request was filed on February 2, 2017, I walked into the building for mediation, hoping that this would be the end of our quest for justice. We were ushered into a conference room where the mediator introduced himself and told us he didn't expect the process to take very long because he knew the insurance company's attorney had come with a restitution number he was authorized to offer. He also told me that there was no dollar amount that would ever fix what had happened to me.

The mediator left and was gone for about an hour and came back looking bewildered. He said the insurance company was claiming that they had not acted in bad faith and that we were at an impasse. He asked me and Chad to step out of the room for a minute, so he could talk to our lawyers. We sat there in the lobby for nearly an hour, watching through the glass window of the conference room as the attorneys talked.

At one point, I was staring at the floor when I felt heat on my cheeks and felt like someone was staring at me. When I looked up, I saw an older man in casual dress walking out of the office. Chad told me it was X's dad. A few minutes later, X walked in front of us, just 10 feet away. I stopped breathing. Chad pulled me close and started rocking me back and forth, repeating over and over again, "He can't hurt you. He can't hurt you." I buried my face in Chad's shoulder. After Chad told me X passed by us again, I finally lifted my head and uncurled my body. When Paul came out of the office, Chad told him what had happened. Paul apologized and moved us into another conference room where I began to blankly stare out the window. I felt myself drifting away, but I was able to use the tools I had learned from Dr. Barngrover to pull myself back. Despite the encounter with X, I felt strong.

At 5:30, a visibly frustrated Paul came in and told us we were done. The other side would rather take their chances at trial. This had simply been an exercise to "call our bluff" to see if we had the stamina to follow this course of action through to the end. We were about to show them we did.

Chad

I walked into the mediation office, nervous and scared but focused. I wasn't sure what to expect, but I was hopeful that this could be the end of this long journey. However, as the hours dragged on, it became clear that the insurance company was not interested in actually negotiating. It felt like they were purposely making us wait, pushing us to the edge to see if we would fold. It was clearly not about fairness; it was about control.

When we were sitting in the lobby and X's dad passed us, I wondered where he was going. Then X himself walked by. I wanted to punch him, but I knew Jess seeing him was the real problem. She froze. I pulled her close and simply repeated, "He can't hurt you" over and over again. The only thing I cared about was making her feel safe.

I was so angry that the insurance company was using tactics that played on Jess's trauma. They knew her history, they knew what she had endured, yet they still pushed those buttons on purpose. I still don't understand how someone does that then goes home to their family and when asked "How was work today?" can answer, "Great, I spent the day making a sexual assault victim relive her fears so the company can save money." That may not be how the insurance company representatives see it, but that's what it felt like to me.

When Paul finally came out and told us they had decided not to settle, I felt discouraged for a moment. This never-ending nightmare would continue. But the more I thought about it, the more determined I became. The other side was trying to see if we had the strength to keep moving forward. We were about to prove to them that we did.

Jessi

In the middle of all of the mediation and trial prep, I lost my job – again. In January, my company notified me that it would be going out of business. I once again found myself on the hunt for a new job. But I was exhausted. The civil suit was emotionally draining as I relived the attack over and over again for the court proceedings. I needed a break, but I refused to allow myself to think about taking one. I had been working since I was 14. I worked all through college, getting a couple of hours between classes. Despite my exhaustion, I updated my resume and started applying.

I hadn't found anything by mid-February when I had lunch with Anne, one of the women in our church small group with whom I had quickly become good friends. Over lunch she shared with me about one of her co-workers deciding to take six months off to do some "soul searching." When she said that, an indescribable feeling of relief washed over me. It felt like a sign from God. On my way home, I called Chad and shared the experience and the idea that I would like to take some time off. I told him I would keep networking and looking for jobs, but he asked me a simple question, "Why are you trying to justify this?"

Chad immediately understood what I was trying to convince myself of. That I needed time to heal. I needed to take the time I hadn't taken in the immediate aftermath of the rape to focus on me and my needs. I was finally ready to give myself permission and space to heal. I would spend the next six months volunteering, writing, and focusing on my home and my health. It would turn out to be one of the most important things I had ever done for myself.

Chad

When Jess talked about taking some time off, I was all in. She had been through so much for so long, and she deserved a break. I knew she would not be sitting on the couch doing nothing. That's not who Jess is.

She took an active break where she could focus on the things that would help her heal. She didn't need to be in a job setting, worrying about the next step in her career. She was worn down and needed time to rest and recharge, not to jump into the next thing just because it was there. My career was stable, so Jess could take this time to focus on herself, on rebuilding who she was and deciding who she wanted to be.

Truthfully, I didn't look at this time as something that would decide her future. I just wanted her to give herself time and grace to let the process of healing take place. Looking back on that time now, I can see that for her, it was a time to slow down and start letting herself live again.

THE TRIAL

"

You don't get a pass for drinking and using that as an excuse for not knowing which bedroom you are in or whatever the excuse is. He didn't deserve a pass, shouldn't get a pass.

Paul

Jessi

Three days before the civil trial was to start, Paul called and told us the judge assigned to our case had changed. We had felt really good about our original judge, so this came as something of a shock. However, Paul felt confident with the new judge and advised us to move forward. If we had challenged the new judge's assignment, we would lose our court date, and it could take a long time to get back on the court's schedule.

On Monday, March 27, 2017, Chad and I walked through the front doors of the 16th Circuit Courthouse of Jackson County, Missouri. Our day in court had finally arrived.

While I was relieved that day had finally come, I was more than nervous. That morning, I was stressed about what I needed to wear. Paul had given us some guidelines–professional with minimal jewelry–but I kept thinking about how the judge would be looking at me and making assumptions about the case based on my appearance. While that might seem silly or shallow to some people, the reality is that studies show how a rape victim dresses does create unconscious bias in juries. Before the late 1970s and early 1980s and the advent of rape shield laws that prohibit the defense from bringing up a victim's past sexual encounters in court unless they are directly relevant to the crime, courts would allow the defense to introduce evidence of how a rape victim was dressed at the time of the crime to argue that the victim's dress implied sexual consent. While that evidence is no longer allowed in court, the unconscious bias against a woman who dresses in a way that accents her sexual attributes is still prevalent in courtrooms. Without consciously thinking about it, my laser focus on what I wore into court reflected my concern about that bias. It's just one more way that our society makes getting justice for sexual assault difficult.

In addition to focusing my nervous energy into worry about what I was wearing, I was also terrified of seeing X again. I stressed about how I was supposed to answer the questions. While Paul was never worried about what answers we would give and told us to just focus on telling the truth, I knew that words could be misconstrued. I wanted to make sure that I stuck to the truth, answered directly, and delivered my testimony with emotion without being disrespectful. Despite the months spent getting ready for this day, it felt like no amount of preparation was enough. But through my nerves, I knew one thing was true: I was ready to face him and to tell everyone what we had been through.

One of the first people I saw when we rounded the corner and headed to our assigned courtroom was a woman sitting on a bench looking at me with a soft smile on her face. I didn't recognize her, but she seemed to know me. Paul seemed to know her, as well. He greeted her then asked if I remembered her and introduced her as Nurse Krieger, the nurse who had done the rape kit at Centerpoint. I didn't remember her. In my mind, it was as if she was a foggy outline of a person. I shook her hand and apologized for not remembering her before continuing on to the courtroom.

We took our place on the right side of the courtroom, directly behind our two lawyers and a legal assistant, watching as the defense lawyers and others filed in. Behind us sat three of our friends who had come for moral support, including my friend Anne.

I was tense and anxious, but knowing that I had people on my side put me more at ease. No matter what happened in this courtroom, my story would be public. People would know what had happened to me, to our family.

The only person who hadn't shown up was X. The time arrived for the trial to start, but there was no sign of him. His attorney informed our legal team that X had mistakenly gone to another courthouse and would be late. X's lawyer requested that the trial proceed without him, and X would arrive during Nurse Krieger's testimony.

There would be no jury in our trial, just a judge. Paul had helped us decide on this option for a variety of reasons. First, Paul was confident a judge would render a favorable verdict and damage award while the choice also limited options for appeals and would save time in collecting damages. In addition, trying the case before a judge eliminated some of the worry that a jury would buy into the defense's argument and would diminish the value of the harm done to us. And last, a trial in front of a judge meant the judge would make findings of fact and conclusions of law that would be a permanent record against X.

Paul's opening statement laid out the facts of the case. X's lawyers were planning to argue that the rape was "unintentional," that X had simply had too much to drink and ended up in the wrong bedroom with the wrong woman. To counter this, at the end of his opening statement, Paul said:

> "Drinking to the point that you're unaware of your surroundings to that extent is a failure to exercise ordinary care. And drinking to the point that your judgment is impaired to the point that you would go into the wrong bedroom and attempt to have sexual relationships with somebody other than your wife is a failure to exercise

ordinary care. Drinking does not give him a pass. He must be held responsible and accountable and at the end of this case we're going to ask you to do that."

The rest of the trial was a seemingly never-ending list of people telling what they knew about the night I relive in my nightmares. I saw X's deposition for the first time, and despite him pleading the fifth to every question, just listening to the questions brought back all the horror and fear of that night. It seemed to go on and on. "Did you knowingly and willingly have intercourse with Jessica Bixler? Did you enjoy having intercourse with Jessica Bixler?"

I had promised myself that I would be strong enough to sit through this trial even though Paul had said I could step outside at any time. I remained in my seat, but after less than an hour, I began to shrink into myself. When Chad took the stand, I listened to most of his testimony until Paul asked me to leave the court-room so Chad could answer questions about our relationship and me without inadvertently hurting me. Those friends that had been sitting at my back came with me, so I wouldn't be alone. Their support meant everything to me. These were people who had chosen to sit with me through the worst, to hear my nightmare laid out in court, simply because they were my friends. Words don't exist to express my thankfulness for them.

That support got me back into the courtroom where it was my turn on the stand. I sat down and stared at my shaking, sweaty hands throughout my testimony. Paul gently walked me through the questions, which I answered as clearly as I could, sobbing as I walked through the events of that night yet again. Once I had got-ten through the details of the actual attack, I began to feel stronger, empowered. I had told the truth about what had happened to me, and while I had been bent nearly in half, I had not broken. I would come out of this a stronger person. At one point, I even looked directly at X. I wanted him to see me as a strong woman, that he hadn't broken or destroyed me. Not once did he look directly at me.

X did not appear to be too engaged in the proceedings. At one point during the trial, one of Paul's team members passed him sticky note that read, "Is that asshole asleep?" X never took the stand, and, in fact, his lawyers and the insurance company's lawyers did not present a defense. In their closing arguments, his attorneys would argue that there was no evidence that X planned to come into our bedroom for a sexual purpose and suggested that X's unfamiliarity with the house combined with his drinking had led to his "unintentional" actions. The attorney also tried to downplay the rape because only touch DNA was found during the rape kit.

Paul's closing argument focused on holding X accountable for his actions, regardless of whether he had had too much to drink:

"Full justice and accountability is absolutely mandated in this case, otherwise it makes her life and her family's life basically worthless. It makes her powerless to protect herself. And it makes women everywhere – whenever there is not justice for something like this, it makes women everywhere powerless. It demeans them and justice just cannot tolerate such a result. Whenever any person is -- whenever any person is wronged, they must hear the bell of justice. And when the bell of justice is rung, the judge will correct whatever wrong has been done. That is what justice is all about."

He closed out our case with these words to rebut the defense's argument:

"You don't get a pass for drinking and using that as an excuse for not knowing which bedroom you are in or whatever the excuse is. He didn't deserve a pass, shouldn't get a pass, and we want you -- and we are asking you or praying that you render a judgment that sends a message to him that he has got to pay for all the harm, not just part of it, the full compensation. Because he'll walk out of this courtroom and she will live with this and Chad will live with this and their family will live with this forever and ever and it is emblazoned on their life in a way that has been traumatic and will never go away."

Chad

I woke up on the morning of the trial so nervous I could feel it my stomach. I was a wreck. This mattered so much. When it was my turn to testify, I was so scared I would freeze up on the stand and not be able to talk or would give an answer that made no sense. I kept thinking I might hear the question wrong and give a stupid answer that would hurt our case.

When I finally sat on the witness stand, the thing that stood out the most was how alone I felt. Everyone I knew left the courtroom to be with Jess when it was my turn. My parents had never shown up. The only person who stayed that I knew was on my side was Anne, and I will be forever grateful to her for that. It made all the difference to have someone in the audience that I knew believed me and was there for me. I'll never forget the feeling of sitting in that box by myself, carrying the entire weight of everything that had happened to us.

Anne

My husband and I met Jess and Chad when we decided to show up to their community group through our church. I was pregnant with our second child and had suffered through a bought of postpartum depression with our first, so we wanted to get plugged in somewhere and make some friends who were in the same stage of life as we were. We looked at all the community group leaders and did some Internet stalking. When we saw pictures of Jess and Chad tailgating at a Chiefs game, we knew that these could be our people. Jess and I hit it off immediately. The moment I met Jess, I knew that we'd have a ride or die type friendship.

We had only known each other six months when it was time for the trial. Jess had shared briefly what had happened to her, but I didn't really know how to talk to her about it. I wanted to be someone who could empathize with her situation, not just sympathize, but I also didn't want to interrupt her healing process by making her talk about things she wasn't ready to talk about.

I was trying to find a place where I could connect with what she was going through versus saying, "I'm so sorry you went through that." Being sorry is entirely different from being empathetic. I wanted her to know "I'm here with you in these trenches of this trauma and grief and emotion that you're going through." That's what I knew Jess needed as a friend versus "I'm really sorry you have this trial coming up. Good luck." I also struggled to decide if I should insert myself into something so heavy, so personal because we were still new friends. I didn't know how that would be received. I was constantly juggling how much to push and how involved to get.

I debated for a long time about whether or not I should attend the trial. I asked Jess what she wanted, and she was noncommittal in her response. Honestly, I don't think she knew what she needed. Another friend of ours had this overwhelming sense that we needed to show up. We're going. We're showing up for her in these trenches.

I wasn't prepared for what I would hear at the trial. I knew Jess had been through a traumatic sexual assault, but I didn't know the details. It was such an eye-opening experience. I remember sitting there, thinking "Holy shit. This is bad. This is fucking horrible." Sitting with her parents and feeling their grief and helplessness while X sat in the courtroom showing no remorse, no emotion, was one of the hardest things I've had to do. When you experience an actual trial and hear how horrific the situation was, you begin to understand the ripple, the downstream effect and how it impacted her entire life, her family, her marriage, her kids; it made it all more real.

There were many things I wasn't prepared for sitting in that courtroom, one of those was witnessing Chad's testimony. It was so raw, and I remember feeling immense grief for him. It became clear that this terrible experience had not only affected Jess but also rippled through her entire family. In that moment, I realized for the first time that Chad was a survivor, too. I saw firsthand that he was grieving as well.

As I listened to the entire day of testimony, I felt sick — and angry. It was really hard not to jump over the barricade and attack

X. It was hard to be in such close proximity to somebody capable of doing what he did. He never once showed remorse for blowing up their life.

Showing up for the trial was one of the most important things I've ever done. I had known Jess for six months, and that one action solidified our friendship in ways that nothing else could. Walking hand in hand with a friend, a survivor, through a traumatic trial experience like that brings you closer than you could ever imagine. I feel honored that I was a part of that, and I'd do it all over again in a heartbeat.

While I hate that this happened to Jess, I love how God brought us together in the aftermath. The biggest thing I've learned about friendship in the wake of something like this is that as a friend, just show up even when you think they might not want you there. Show up and ask questions, even if they seem uncomfortable. If they're not ready to talk, you'll know. In those moments, when talking doesn't come easily, sit with them in their grief, never losing faith that someday you'll get to dance with them in their healing.

Jessi

The judge had heard all the evidence, and it was time for his judgment. We took a recess for the judge to consider the case, and Chad and I waited in a small room around the corner from the courtroom. Paul would check in with us periodically, and after an hour, he came in to tell us the judge was ready. I was nervous and didn't know whether to feel relieved or worried that it had taken the judge such a short amount of time to reach a judgment.

I entered the courtroom on unsteady feet. After all the testimony and the closing arguments, my body felt empty, weak, and wobbly. I stared intently at the judge, praying that he would find in our favor. I didn't know what I would do if he didn't.

The judge began:

"Here in Division 15 we have the honor and the privilege of trying a lot of lawsuits. And [the court reporter] and I have heard a lot of victims in a lot of criminal proceedings testify about horrendous facts and horrendous actions that they have been put through. We hear the human condition on a daily basis. We hear it on a regular basis. I don't know though that in all those criminal proceedings, all those sentences that we've heard, that I've heard a more compelling, poignant, gut-wrenching recitation of a traumatic event as I've heard here today. Not only from Jessica, but also from Chad and also from the Mells."

I clutched Chad's hand so tightly that I'm sure he lost feeling in his fingers. This judge held our story in his hands. We had told our story, and he had not only believed us but had felt the weight of what we had shared. The judge's words seemed to be in our favor, but I was still nervous. It seemed the judge not only understood that the event itself had been traumatic, he voiced the terrible reality that the effects of the assault would continue after we left his courtroom.

"You know, what occurs to me through the testimony as to what I've heard is that that trauma is going to continue, unfortunately. That gut-wrenching narrative that I heard today is something that is going to continue for Lord knows how long. And it's my only hope that you find some closure and some healing somewhere down the road. I know it's going to be a long haul. Like I said, [X's lawyer] is a wonderful lawyer who I respect a great deal. And I know he was advocating for his client. But what occurred in that house that night was at the very least the heighth of negligence. And I'm not fully convinced it wasn't something else. But it certainly was the heighth of an egregious act of negligence."

The judge was clear in his belief that my story was true, which was vindicating for me.

"How [X] ended up in that room I think only he knows. But as far as the act itself, what transpired inside that room, again, I find Jessica's testimony convincing, poignant, and again incredibly compelling. And I add to the fact that [X] utilized the protections afforded him under the Fifth Amendment, which is his absolute right, but in a civil case that comes with a price, as we all know. And that price is an adverse inference. So at the very least I'm going to find that I have no evidence before me that is going to rebut what Jessica said occurred in that room. And that just adds to my conviction that something horrible happened in that room. Sexual assault, rape, call it what you will, but it was an uninvited, unwarranted, unsolicited, unimaginable, violative intrusion on her most precious parts, and it's something that I just can't imagine."

In addition, the judge was sympathetic about the damage caused to not just me, but to my entire family.

"Add to that the collateral damage, not only to Jessica herself, but also to Chad and their relationship, which is just astoundingly horrendous as far as I'm concerned, and to the Mells, the parents, who now have a daughter who is inconsolable. That all is horrific, but what brings me to my knees and wrenches my gut the most is the kids. The damage to those kids, [her daughter], who will forever attach her birthday, it will be clouded by this horrendous event. And again, it's my hope that somehow, some way, and I don't know if it's possible, but if there's somehow, some way you can diminish that cloud and take it away so that she can enjoy birthdays some time in the future going forward. And [her son], man, it's my only hope that he's as strong a kid as his name suggests, because the fact that he thinks he needs to protect his mommy at this young age is just again gut-wrenching to me. They lost a parent that they used to know. And [her daughter] only had the benefit of having her for one year. And so it's truly my hope that as time goes on those wounds will heal. That's the tragedy in all this. That's the gut-wrenching part. That's the part that tears at your heart and really does bring you to your knees."

The judge had also noticed X's lack of engagement in the proceedings and had some harsh words for him:

"And I would be remiss if I didn't say that, again, I have the utmost respect for [X's lawyer], but [X], you seemed completely disinterested here today and almost amused by some of the testimony as I was watching you during the course of the day. Disinterested, remorseless, contritionless, and you know, I don't know if that is a defense mechanism of yours or not, but it was certainly off-putting to me because this is an event, if it doesn't tear you to pieces, I don't know if you're human."

Then came the words we had been waiting for:

"Having said all that, I am going to find all issues in favor of the plaintiffs on all issues."

We were done. After our previous disappointment with the criminal justice system, having a judge believe me gave me a feeling of validation that so many rape survivors never get to experience. I burst into tears and hugged Chad, Paul and my parents. I know it was difficult for my parents to relive the events of that night and its aftermath, but it meant so much to me that they came to support me and Chad. Our reaction probably looked like a scene out of a movie. X's lawyer came over and apologized and wished us well. All I felt was relief. Now, we could finally move on, and the judgment we had sought would be publicly issued, forever attaching X's name to the assault.

Chad

When it was over, all I felt was relief. This judge was unbiased. He had seen so many cases and knew how to look at evidence and make a decision. To hear him say he believed us and acknowledge everything we had been through was a huge victory. But while I was happy the judge had found in our favor, no amount of compensation was ever going to repair the wrong that had been done to us. Our lives had been shattered, and we were still slowly putting them back together. Looking back on the trial now, I feel relieved and blessed. It was hard to testify, to bear the weight of that loneliness and responsibility as I told my story, but it needed to be done, and I'm glad I did it.

Jessi

The trial ended around 5 p.m. Chad's parents picked up our kids from daycare and met us at a Mexican restaurant for dinner. Because we had the kids with us, we didn't really talk too much about the case. Mostly, they asked who was there, what it was like, and if the judge was wearing "a robe and all that garb." Our kids had no idea what was going on, but I felt lighter. Even though I knew we still had steps to take to receive the judgment, the hardest part was over. This dinner was a celebration. I had faced X in court and verbalized what *he* did to our family when at the time of the rape, X's wife had been so worried about what *we* were doing to the family.

In all those lawyer shows on TV, justice is swift. We see the judgment delivered, and the plaintiff walks out of the courtroom jubilant. We assume that they receive whatever judgment they are owed and move on with their lives. In reality, the justice system works very differently. The judge had awarded us a settlement, but we still had to go through the proper legal channels to receive that compensation, which required another round of mediation, which would drag on into 2019. The second round of mediation was aimed at getting the insurance company to pay out the judgment because we had to prove that they were liable to pay the damages.

However, just the thought of another mediation session made me nervous.

When we went for mediation, we were tucked away in a conference room at the back of Paul's office. With the memory of the last mediation still fresh in my mind, I went into this one unwilling to be jerked around. When the mediator entered the room with an offer so low it was insulting, I felt like something erupted inside me. Words came rushing out of my mouth with no filter. The mediator decided to step out of the office and let us talk with Paul, who asked me to explain what I was feeling despite it being pretty obvious from the tirade I had gone on with the mediator in the room. I realized I had not thought before speaking, so I took a minute to breathe and more calmly told Paul that I felt as if X's side was trying to take advantage of us. They were trying to get away with giving us the bare minimum. I knew this was the lawyer's job, but this time it felt personal. Despite the judge siding with us, it was like they were trying to ignore the judgment, ignore everything that had been said, to invalidate the pain and chaos this event had created in our lives. I was done being silent and doing things the "right" way. I would be heard.

Paul agreed. He encouraged us to make a single "take it or leave it" offer, which we did. The other party accepted. The next time the mediator came in, he had the terms written up on a yellow legal pad.

When I signed it, I looked at Paul with tears clouding my eyes and asked, "Are we done?"

"We are done."

I pressed again, "Like, done-done?"

"Yes, done-done."

I let my head fall into my arms on the table and sobbed — loud, messy, snotty sobs with hiccups mixed in. I felt Chad's hand rub my back gently, steadying me. When I finally lifted my head, I saw tears in Paul's eyes too.

Jessi

For the first few days after the trial, I was elated. I couldn't get the smile off my face, and I felt like I was skipping through the days. It was as if a weight had been lifted off my shoulders. But the more days that passed, the less happy I felt. In fact, I felt hollow and empty. It was as if my mind and soul were playing a game of pinball, bouncing from happiness to emptiness within minutes. I was looking toward the future, beginning to explore advocacy for sexual assault survivors, but I still couldn't put the feeling of emptiness aside.

In addition, I still had so much anger inside of me. I think I really thought the trial would help me to release those feelings. I would get some form of justice and be able to move forward. But justice isn't a magic wand that provides healing. It's just a step in the process. I found myself lashing out at my kids when they were fighting or becoming enraged when their toys weren't in the right place. I wanted to run away and destroy something just to let the anger out.

I remember one instance being furious with Chad's mom, Julie, when she defended Chad's cousin's wife for posting that photo of X and his family with them on Facebook. Apparently, Chad's cousin had sent Julie an apology text the next day after taking down the photo, but it felt to me like Chad's parents were giving his cousin a pass for letting a rapist into their house. Another time, Julie had voiced her sympathy for X's wife's parents, telling us that they felt awful about what had happened. I lost my temper and said, "How do you know? They have never called Chad or I to tell us that, or to ask how we were doing. They still allow that disgusting human being in their home and their daughter to remain with him and be subjected to God knows what." It just felt like people were making excuses for family members because they didn't want to rock the boat.

While my anger was justified, it was still getting in the way of my healing, so on April 24, one month after the trial, I went to see Dr. Barngrover to get some help dealing with the roller coaster of emotions. I felt grateful that I had these months off from work to get ready for the trial, but now I had crossed that finished line only to be confronted with a long road in front of me. I had no idea which turn to take to decide what I wanted to do with the rest of my life. It just felt like I was searching for something more.

Dr. Barngrover asked me if I had ever heard of the Parable of the Sower from the Bible. I had not. She told me that a farmer began by planting his crops with seeds on the surface of the dirt. That harvest yielded very little crop due to the birds eating the seeds or the wind simply blowing them away. The next year he planted the seeds beneath the surface of the dirt. While he produced a larger crop compared to the past year, he was not yet satisfied. So the following year he dug deeper into the dirt and planted the seeds. His harvest this year produced more than he knew what to do with. He began to see that he had given his plants the opportunity to root down deep and flourish from within. She then asked me what I was planting within me and allowing to establish roots?

I was speechless. Wasn't all this time off meant for me to redesign the kind of life that I wanted? I suddenly realized that I had spent so much time doing that I hadn't left any room to fill myself up, to continue to heal. There had been no chance to plant anything deep within my soul and give it a chance to grow and flourish. I had been searching for the next thing to do instead of the next thing to plant.

Jessi

Armed with the realization that I needed to start nurturing my soul and not just filling my days with things to do, I met with Dawn, another one of my close friends, who encouraged me to set aside time in my week for healing and reflection. She helped me to set up my week so I would devote Mondays, Wednesdays, and Fridays to "work" tasks while leaving Tuesdays and Thursdays open to focus on healing, reflection, and mom/wife duties.

With time for reflection, I began to understand that my desire to continue to climb the corporate ladder had disappeared. I learned that I wanted to help people on a larger scale and that the things that I thought were important had changed. On one of my "reflection days," I made a list of the things that were important to me now:

- Flexibility to participate in and help out at my children's school
- Time to travel
- Work from home or less than 20-minute commute
- Maintain eight hours of sleep per night
- Consistent work-out and yoga schedule
- Love what I do; make a difference
- Help others accomplish a goal or meet a need

- Stand up against sexual violence
- Financial stability
- Low stress
- Strong faith in God
- Solid group of friends

When I looked at this list, I still didn't know exactly what the path forward looked like, but I felt I could start taking small steps. One of those steps was to get certified as a Holy Yoga instructor. From the very beginning, yoga had played a large role in my healing process, and I had begun to regularly attend a Holy Yoga class at our church. Holy Yoga uses the same poses as traditional yoga, but the mental focus is on God and "the person you are becoming in Christ." I completed the certification through self-led coursework, virtual classes, and Bible studies then attended a weeklong in-person camp with hundreds of other instructors. It was a powerful process that challenged my faith and forced me into a deeper understanding of what it means to walk with Jesus.

My family was supportive of my decision to become a Holy Yoga instructor, especially my son who offered to make me a sign for people to put money in a jar and suggested that I start a yoga club at his school even though he knew some of the boys wouldn't want to participate. His enthusiasm was a balm to my wounded and weary heart.

I also decided it was time to use my experience to help other people, so shortly after the trial, I reached out to the Metropolitan Organization Countering Sexual Assault (MOCSA) to see how I could get involved. I met with a MOCSA representative to tell her my story and talk about my interests. We agreed I should join the Young at Art committee, the planning committee for MOCSA's fall cocktail event, the organization's second-largest fundraiser of the year. This event seemed like the easiest way to get my feet wet because I love party planning and figuring out how to connect people emotionally to an event. I also signed up to complete the 40-hour volunteer training in July that year that included a two-day in-person training with a MOCSA staff member and volunteers. I declined to participate in the training's visit to a local hospital to see an exam room and meet with a SANE nurse. I wasn't ready for that and did not think that I would ever be part of the hospital activation team.

As I took these small steps forward, I could begin to see a life that would never fully put what had happened to me behind us but one that could use the strength and resilience I had gained to help others process their own trauma. I will never be thankful that I was assaulted, but I was beginning to glimpse a time when I could be thankful for the person I would become because I had put in the work to begin healing, allowed myself time and space to reflect, and used the strength I had gained to put that healing and those reflections into action.

STARTING A BUSINESS

"

I could see her potential even when
she was second-guessing herself.

Chad

Jessi

I was coming up on the six month mark of losing my job, and while I was making progress on allowing myself to heal, I hadn't taken a lot of steps forward on what I wanted to do next professionally. But then my friend Dawn, the same one who had helped me set up a schedule that allowed time for reflection and healing, asked me to help her with some marketing for her new consulting business. I jumped at the chance, considering it a chance to help a friend and give my skills a workout.

As I worked with Dawn designing her website to support her vision, I remembered that I loved doing this. As soon as I dove into her branding and understood her plans for the future, I could see the pieces of her website coming together in my mind. Putting those pieces together gave me a sense of satisfaction that I didn't get from any other piece of my life. While we were working together, Dawn introduced me to another friend of hers who was also starting her own business and needed a website. Without really meaning to, I was building up a clientele.

Dawn worked with me and mentored me over the next couple of months to help me learn what I needed to know to start my own small business. She taught me how to charge for my services, write contracts, and develop my business. She encouraged me to chart my own path.

I had never really thought too much about running my own business before this. I had always thought when I was ready I would simply go find a job working for someone else, but when I looked at the list of things that were important to the post-assault me, climbing the corporate ladder was no longer on the list. If I wanted flexibility that gave me time to pursue my new ideals and goals, then working for myself seemed like the best option.

I spent a lot of time talking to Chad as we took walks that summer. He encouraged me to try it and was instrumental in helping me make a number of decisions to move forward with the process. After all we had been through, it was nice to be able to focus on taking steps forward together instead of being hyper-focused on the events of the past.

On August 11, 2017, almost exactly six months from when I had decided to take a break, Bixler Consulting was formed. I was officially a business owner.

Chad

I was so excited for Jess to start her business. She was finally going to experience entrepreneurship for herself, and it was something that we could work on together. I already ran my own business, so I was happy to share my experience with her to help her get started. I had no concerns that she would not be successful. She had the skills, persistence, and resilience it takes to succeed. In addition, we were in a good place financially, so she could have the time she needed to get things off the ground without worrying about needing to turn a profit right away. It felt like the perfect time for her to step out on her own.

I loved that it gave her something to focus her time and attention on in a way that was allowing her to build something new. So much of our lives had been about what was broken, but this was an opportunity to create something beautiful out of the broken pieces. I was excited to see her build a business that both helped people and made money. I could see her potential even when she was second-guessing herself. I felt blessed to be able to help her grow and flourish.

MOCSA

"

I had gone from a rape victim who had thrown MOCSA's card in the trash as soon as she arrived from the hospital to one of their biggest advocates.

Jessi

Jessi

Over the next nine months, I settled into running and growing my business, made it through another anniversary of the rape, taught yoga, and continued volunteering with MOCSA. Being able to see that my trauma could help others going through the same thing truly helped me to heal and become more whole, so when Terry asked me to come to a meeting to talk about me joining the board, I readily agreed.

Terry had been my boss at The Kansas City Business Journal, which is where I heard about MOCSA for the first time, many years before I was assaulted. Our publisher at the time sat on MOCSA's board, and I remember when I first heard about what MOCSA did, I was surprised at the depth of the need for MOCSA's services. During the time I was trying to figure out my next steps after the trial, I had lunch with another former co-worker and friend, Stacie, who mentioned that Terry was now on MOCSA's board and that MOCSA might be a great place to start investing some of my time.

Prior to joining the board in January 2019, I got involved with MOCSA's speaker's bureau and began telling my story to strangers during lunch and learns and other corporate events, emphasizing the need for MOCSA's services. Being able to share my story publicly was a big step, and it's one many sexual assault survivors never take. There is no one right path forward after a rape. Everyone heals in their own way, but my way was to take control of the story, to control my own narrative.

Over the years, I have served in a variety of ways at MOCSA. From serving on the Marketing and Fund Development Committee my first year on the board to being the voice of survivors as the Survivor Speaker for MOCSA's Community Luncheon, a single event open to about 1,000 people, to heading up the Board of Directors as board chair. I had gone from a rape victim who had thrown MOCSA's card in the trash as soon as she arrived home from the hospital to one of their biggest advocates. I had learned that MOCSA didn't have to be a sexual assault survivor's first call. The organization would be there whenever survivors were ready to engage.

One of my favorite events that I got to participate in as part of MOCSA was in 2021. MOCSA had been named as the three-year recipient for the Kansas City Chiefs Charity Game, the first pre-season game of the year where the Chiefs help to raise funds for a local charity. I was chosen to represent survivors as the drum honoree for that game, a tradition where a local "celebrity" beats the Chiefs' giant drum during warm-ups to energize the fans. The next year, my kids were designated "kids of the game" and got to go on the field during warm-ups, high five the players as they went to the locker room, receive game balls from Patrick Mahomes and custom jerseys with their names on the back. These perks were fun but also helped to draw attention to MOCSA's mission.

My time on the board has also given my kids a chance to see me retake control of my life. I don't really know how much they remember about the early days after the rape. They were so small, so probably not much, but the assault changed my interactions with them. Even now, I still get irrationally scared at times or something will trigger my emotions. I can be angry for no reason. Kids pick up on that even if they don't know the reason why, so when my son recently joined me at the Community Luncheon, he got to see his mom, healthy and strong, welcome people to an event designed to raise awareness and money to help survivors like me.

But my joining the board of MOCSA wasn't just about fun experiences and being an example for my kids. Real changes have been made at MOCSA to better their interactions with sexual assault survivors in the six years since my first contact with the organization in an exam room at Centerpoint hospital. Some of those changes include:

1. **Healing bags** – I remember when the MOCSA representative handed me clothes to put on after mine were taken as evidence. They felt like prison attire. I felt like I was marked and everyone who saw me would know something terrible had happened to me. Now, when a survivor receives a healing bag, the MOCSA advocate chooses clothing based on gender and size, and the clothing is much more casual in appearance, allowing survivors to more easily blend in when they leave the exam room. Bags also include underwear and a bra for women as well as toiletry items that give survivors the ability to be clean no matter their current situation.

2. **Advocacy at the hospital** – While I chose not to have a MOCSA advocate with me during the exam, many survivors appreciate the support. Advocates are trained to make sure the survivor always has a choice about whether they want an advocate present. Advocates can provide information about MOCSA and other resources, answer questions about the process at the hospital, give information about the next steps, and provide emotional support. Advocates also often follow up with survivors after the hospital visit.

3. **Advocacy during a police report** – Chad and I were all alone when we gave our statements to the police. In addition to being traumatized, that process was scary. What if we said the wrong thing? We wondered if the police officers were trying to trick us into saying something wrong.

When we filed for the order of protection, an advocate from Hope House walked us through the process, but we had to get to that point on our own. When we met with the prosecutor, an advocate from one of the local agencies was there, but it felt like she was there to protect the prosecutor, not worry about our well-being.

MOCSA advocates are trained to help sexual assault survivors navigate the legal process. They provide information about MOCSA and ongoing services as well as information about outside resources like domestic violence resources and shelters, answer questions about the next steps in the legal process, support the client's needs while questions are being asked (for example, having a signal when the client needs a break), and inform the client that nothing they share with us will be shared with the officers.

4. **Legal services** – We were fortunate to have the means and connections to hire our own attorney, but many people do not. MOCSA offers legal services that can provide legal support for victims, help with orders of protection, navigate visa requirements for immigrants, provide support in custody matters, advocate for victims' rights, and address housing issues.

In addition, MOCSA provides a 24-hour crisis line, counseling, support groups, police and law enforcement advocacy, community and professional education, community prevention programs, and school education programs. The longer I have served as part of MOCSA's board, the more I realize how critical the services that MOCSA, and organizations across the country like MOCSA, provide are to the well-being of sexual assault survivors. While I refused most of MOCSA's services as I dealt with my own trauma, I know that what we do is essential to the health and healing of a survivor in their most vulnerable moment. MOCSA's services don't disappear when you walk out of the hospital. They are there waiting whenever an assault survivor is ready to access them.

Working with MOCSA has been a defining part of my journey in the wake of the assault. There is no one right way to heal from this kind of trauma. Some assault survivors may never be able to speak publicly about what happened to them and working with other survivors may simply complicate their own trauma, but for me, putting my story in the public spotlight has been incredibly empowering. For me, being able to own my story, to put it into words, and to highlight the terrible wrong that was done to me has led to scars finally forming open wounds. It has given me a purpose that I didn't have in the wake of the assault. Although I pushed MOCSA's help away in the immediate aftermath, it would be MOCSA that helped to heal my soul.

LIVER FAILURE

- 2018 -

"

After day three or four with
no answers and Jess getting
progressively worse, I was
beginning to lose hope. That was
definitely my lowest point.

Chad

Jessi

In September 2018, I had just celebrated the first year anniversary of Bixler Consulting, which was growing by word of mouth and referrals. In that year, I had not only learned a lot about running a small business, but I had also continued to make progress in my healing. Our faith was growing as we regularly met with our small group, and our lives were starting to feel more normal. While I still saw Dr. Barngrover regularly, our visits had become less frequent except for the months around the anniversary of the assault. We had deepened our friendships with our community group members, and I was beginning to look forward more often than I looked back.

One night when we were hosting small group, I was so tired I could barely keep my eyes open despite the nearly dozen people in my home. I had been slightly nauseous throughout the past few weeks, but I chalked it up to being hungry since I wasn't great about eating on a schedule. I had noticed an orange tint to my urine, but I simply thought I was dehydrated and made a mental note to drink more water. That night, I thought maybe I was coming down with a bug and brushed off my exhaustion as nothing.

A few days later on October 2, I looked in the mirror and did a double take. I leaned in and opened my eyes wide. The whites of my eyes were yellow. I blinked and looked again. Still yellow. I called Chad and had him look, and he agreed that they had a yellow tinge to them. Still thinking it was probably nothing, we agreed to go to urgent care just to be safe. We dropped our kids at mid-week kids church and headed to urgent care, certain that we would be done in time to pick them up.

They took us back to an exam room, and a nurse came in. He had me open my eyes wide and shined a light in them before quickly switching off the light and telling us we needed to go straight to the emergency room. He refused to say any more about what he thought might be wrong with me, just that they couldn't treat me at the urgent care. We were shocked. I figured at most I had some kind of infection that could be treated with antibiotics.

We ended up at Lee's Summit Medical Center and got in quickly. Nurses took a urine and blood sample. When the tests came back, my liver enzymes were out of sight. My AST was 709 (normal is 10-45), and my ALT was 1,046 (normal is 12-78). My bilirubin, which is produced when your body breaks down old red blood cells, was 4.2 (normal is 0-1). They also did a CT scan that showed nothing malignant, which was a relief. They admitted me overnight and started an IV to deal with some slight dehydration. Our friends David and Natalie picked up our kids and kept them overnight.

My levels continued to be high, and the doctors ran a smorgasbord of tests, including a liver biopsy to check for cancer, which came back negative. They did MRIs, blood tests to check for everything from hepatitis to rocky mountain spotted fever. They needed so much blood that they put a PICC line in so they didn't have to stab me so many times, which was difficult for Chad because we had nearly lost his mom when she contracted sepsis from having a PICC line put in. Thankfully, mine went in without any complications.

Chad was making frequent trips to the hospital while the kids were at school and trying to keep everything running smoothly at home, and we couldn't have made it through without the help from our friends. They jumped into help with the kids and made sure I had plenty of visitors in the hospital. In addition, they helped us seek out second opinions from friends and colleagues in the medical field when there was talk of transferring me to a different hospital.

Eventually, the doctors began to talk about the possibility of a liver transplant, and Chad and I began having conversations about what would happen if I never got better. Those discussions were hard. The thought of being chronically ill or even dying was terrifying. We had made it through so much, and this could be how it ended. It seemed so unfair. While I knew that God was in control, it just seemed like our family had already been through so much. And now this. When would we get a break?

The worst moments came when I thought about how all of this was impacting my kids. Chad would call every evening and have the kids FaceTime with me before bed. One night, I was about to say goodbye when my son clapped his hands together and started to pray, "Please God, help my mommy get better." I lost it and started sobbing. He opened his eyes and said, "Why are you crying, Mommy?" I looked at his sweet face and said through my tears, "Because that was so beautiful, buddy."

As my time in the hospital dragged on, my parents came down to help with the kids. I was thankful for the help, but it was also stressful because I knew that they were not getting along and there was tension between them. I asked them to simply tell me what was going on, but I couldn't get a clear answer. I felt my body absorb some of that stress and tension, as well.

At this point, the doctors were stumped. No one could figure out that while my liver readings had decreases slightly, they were remaining stubbornly high. I had one doctor stop by my room and give me her card and asked me to follow up with her when they figured out what was wrong because she had never seen a case like mine. I spent six nights in the hospital and went home without a diagnosis and instructions to follow up with gastroenterology. I was thrilled to be going home, but I was frustrated and exhausted. That six-night stay would wrack up a $100,000 medical bill, and we were no closer to knowing what was wrong with me.

I continued seeing the gastroenterologist over the next few months along with taking a high dose of steroids, which made my whole body swell up. I felt like a balloon, and my eyes felt like there was a film over them. It was miserable, but over the next three months, my numbers slowly came down, and I was able to wean off the medication. Finally, I was back to normal, but no one ever figured out why my liver had gone haywire.

I think the most likely explanation came from Dr. Barngrover who told me she thought it was a manifestation of the trauma I had held in my body for so long. When she testified in court, Dr. Barngrover had discussed how chronic stress can build up in the body of trauma survivors, resulting in medical complications, including GI distress and auto-immune diseases. We can't know for sure that this is what caused this scary episode with my liver, but it seems like the most logical conclusion to me.

Chad

The minute the nurse said we needed to go to the ER, I knew something was seriously wrong. Jess's eyes were yellow, and the look on the doctors' and nurses' faces told me whatever was wrong with her wasn't good.

The hospital stay was rough. I was so scared I might lose her. That thought played in my head over and over again. I never expected to be in my 30s facing the loss of my wife. I thought we had more time. Every time I saw her in the hospital with those IVs hooked up to her arms, getting test after test, my heart sank. After day three or four with no answers and Jess getting progressively worse, I was beginning to lose hope. That was definitely my lowest point.

At home, I simply did what needed to be done. I won't say I managed it well, but I just kept showing up – at the hospital and for the kids. I'm so thankful for all the support from friends and family. There is no way I could have juggled Jess's illness and the kids by myself. People brought meals, got the kids where they needed to go, and did anything else that needed to be done.

When Jess finally came home, I was so relieved. Knowing that for a while it was possible that she might not come home had shaken me to my core. It made every day we have together even more precious.

Jessi

The episode with my liver reminded me that trauma never goes away. You can learn to live with it. You can learn tools to help you through it. But once something traumatic has happened to you, it will always be with you, and your body will remember it. As a yoga instructor, I'm keenly aware of how closely connected the mind and body are. If one is stressed too far, the other will break. I can heal from the assault. My wounds can turn into scars, but the scars will never go away – and they can always break open again.

I'm a stronger person today than I was before the assault. I have walked this road and come through to the other side, but it's not a process that will ever be finished. I will always be healing, and there will always be a trigger that can break through that healing. My body and mind will always remember what was done to me.

For this reason, I try to be as healthy as I can be. I do my best to eat well, exercise, and take care of my mental health because I know that the healthier my mind and body are, the better able they will be to deal with the remnants of trauma that still haunt me today.

It's hard to explain to those who haven't experienced a major trauma what it's like to carry it with you. It's a lot like the story of Sisyphus, the deceitful king of Greek mythology who was doomed to push a boulder up a hill for eternity. Every time he nearly reached the top, it would roll back down, and he would have to start over. Trauma is the boulder, and trauma survivors are continually pushing it back up the hill to keep it from crushing them and their loved ones.

Jessi

When the assault happened, my kids were so little that they didn't know anything about it. They maybe knew that Mommy was sad a lot, but at three and one years old, it wasn't an event that they would even remember. As they got older, though, I knew I would need to tell them about it. I worried incessantly about telling my daughter, whose birthday fell on the day of the assault.

When my son was 12 or 13, I had a persistent feeling that I needed to tell him what had happened. I spoke to Dr. Barngrover about it, and she encouraged me to go ahead and tell my son but to be careful to let him lead the conversation. So, one day on the way to Costco, I started the conversation by asking my son if he knew what MOCSA was and why it was so important. He said no. We talked about what rape was and about what had happened to me. He had so many questions, but he focused in on the fact that X was part of the family. He was so confused.

As a parent, my heart broke. It's one thing to have something happen to you but seeing that trauma now reach out and touch your child in ways that it hadn't before created a special kind of hurt in my momma heart. I wanted to take that pain and confusion away from him. I decided it was time to take a break from the conversation for both of us to process the information. I told him he could always ask questions of me or his dad. When we got home, my son had a few more questions about Chad's side of the family and who knew, then he jumped into my arms and started crying. My heart hurt for him, but I felt incredibly close to him. It was as if a lot of things suddenly made sense to him that hadn't before.

When it came to telling my daughter, I was much more worried than I had been about telling my son. Would this forever ruin her birthday? More than anything, I didn't want that. That was her day, and I didn't want one man's act to forever ruin a day of celebration for her. I took a similar approach to telling my daughter and readied myself for an onslaught of questions. She listened quietly then asked, "Oh, so that's why we don't see Dad's side of the family?" I said yes. She paused, didn't have any other questions and went to bed.

Just as I, Chad, my parents, and my friends had all processed the assault in our own ways, my kids, too, had unique paths to making sense of what had happened in their world at a time when they were too young to remember it.

Jessi

While some of the wounds from the assault may never heal completely, we have made progress on mending some of the broken relationships with Chad's family.

In the spring of 2025, Chad's cousin, whose wife had posted the photo of X on Facebook so many years earlier, sent him a text asking if Chad would be willing to speak with him. Chad agreed. When he called, they made small talk before his cousin began to get emotional and apologized profusely for his wife posting that photo. He explained that at the time of that picture, they knew they were meeting up with Chad's cousin (X's wife) and her son for lunch. They didn't expect X to be there and didn't realize he was until he walked out of the bathroom toward the table they were seated at. They didn't know what to do.

Chad's cousin asked for his forgiveness. Chad immediately gave it. He could tell this had been weighing on his cousin for many years and could almost feel a weight lifted after they got off the call.

A few months later, Chad's mom told us his cousin would be swinging through town on their way to a family reunion. They had asked Chad's mom to invite us over to see them while they were in town. I suggested that Chad take the kids and go without me in case it would be too much for everyone to handle, but he wanted me to go as well.

Leading up to that evening, my kids had many questions about why they had never met this family before. I shared with my son, specifically, that I was feeling a little anxious about the meet-up because it had been so many years since the photo incident, but it was still such a traumatic moment. I said, "It will be fun for everyone else, just awkward for me." My son paused a beat before responding and said, "Well, I'll be there for you." I had to fight back tears. It felt like that moment years ago when he curled up into my lap and offered his protection.

On the evening of the meet-up, I was incredibly nervous, pacing around Chad's parents' house, willing everything to go smoothly. When Chad's cousin and his family showed up, we greeted them at the door, and you could tell we were all hesitant and careful, almost like we were feeling out the edges of a fragile truce. Still, we hugged gently, and as the evening went on, we settled into small talk around the dinner table. The conversation stayed light—family, jobs, kids, the everyday things that feel safe. We all carried the weight of the unspoken, but no one pushed it.

As the night wound down and we began gathering our things to leave, I stepped off to the side, giving space for goodbyes. That's when Chad's cousin walked over, slipped his arm around my shoulder, and leaned in close. His voice caught as he told me how proud he was of Chad and me, of the family we had built, of the children we were raising. Then his composure broke, and tears filled his eyes. He said how deeply sorry he was for the pain his family had caused us all these years, and he asked me for my forgiveness.

Before I could respond, his wife came up quietly and placed her arm around my other shoulder. The three of us stood there, arms linked, tears streaming. It was raw and unpolished—just grief and release and years of silence breaking open. Through the lump in my throat, I told them that I forgave them. In that moment, I realized no one had ever asked me for forgiveness before. It was a profound thing, heavy and yet strangely freeing.

Forgiveness. It's a simple word but one loaded with struggle and emotion. It's an idea I've wrestled with deeply. As a Christian, I know we are called to forgive. But as a human—honestly—I don't believe I will ever be able to forgive X for what he did to me and to my family. That wound runs too deep. Yet over the years, I've learned that forgiving the person and forgiving the act are two different things. I doubt I will ever be able to forgive X the person, but forgiving the act itself would release its hold on my life. Chad helped me understand that without forgiving the rape, I would always be chained to it. It would continue to hold power over me, suffocating the life and future God still had for me.

It wasn't quick. It wasn't easy. But slowly, with time, prayer, and work, I can now say with certainty: the rape no longer holds power over me. Neither does X. That night with Chad's family confirmed something I had been leaning into for years: forgiveness is less about excusing the past and more about reclaiming the future.

I often think of something pastor and author Craig Groeschel said: *"The burden you bear often reveals the calling you'll embrace."* In learning to forgive, I found not only healing, but also my voice, my faith, and my calling.

Friends & Family

I've talked a lot about how I feel like there are two Jessi Bixlers, the one that existed before the assault and the one that I am today. While that was a difficult transition for me, it was especially difficult for my friends and family who had to figure out who I am now and what that means for them. For the most part, my friends and family are just happy that I'm healed enough to be an everyday part of their world again, but I know sometimes they hunger for just a glimpse of the woman they used to know. – Jessi

Mom/Debbie

Jess has been through so much, and I am tremendously proud of her for taking this situation and doing something good with it through her involvement with MOCSA. It's amazing. I don't know that I could do it, but she's been able to do that and get involved in finding ways to help other people with her story. I'm incredibly proud of her for what she's been able to do.

Dad/Tony

Jess is such a loving, caring person and it's a joy to be around her. She just amazes me every day. She's back the way she was.

Fun-loving, happy. She's always on the go. I have a hard time keeping up with her.

Josh

I think that it's like with every obstacle, good can come out of it. I've seen a side of Jess that I never knew existed, and maybe that was partially just because we weren't close, so I never really got to see that. But seeing her strength, I've felt good about seeing how strong she is. She's probably one of the strongest people I know. She's unrattled. It's like you throw something at her, and she's just going to step over it and keep going. I don't think anybody could possibly say that she hasn't become stronger through her own force of will. Unfortunately, it's because she's had to be, and it's not fair that she's had to be.

Aunt Patti

I went to her MOCSA lunch and heard her tell her story. I knew the story. I had heard it. But then I sat there, and I silently watched other people. I watched her husband look at her with admiration. I watched her brother sit up strong and be so proud of her. But then I looked next to me, and I saw a man sitting next to me that didn't know her at all with tears running down his face. So she was impacting more than just her family. She took a terrible tragedy and she continues to make a difference.

Anne

One big thing I've learned is that healing isn't linear, and there's not a day when this is all 'over.' This is a lifetime scar. I've been so honored to have a front row seat to watching Jess embrace that scar, sharing her story for thousands, in an effort to make sure that other survivors know they are not alone in their trauma. I was proud of her then, in that courtroom, and I'm even more proud of her today.

Nancy

I can't even imagine the work that Jess has gone through to come out on the other side of that. I'm just super proud of her. She has gone above and beyond what I ever would have expected. I knew she was going to be okay, but I worried a little bit about her and Chad. It's like she took this and made it a great example of resiliency and strength and faith, and she lives it every day. It's inspiring.

Jessi

As I write this, we are quickly approaching the twelfth anniversary of the assault, a time I still have to mentally prepare myself for each year. Writing this book has given me a chance to look in the mirror and see who I am today compared to the woman I was on the morning of Nov. 30, 2013. Part of me misses that woman and her innocence. She had faced some difficulties, but when she looked at the world, she didn't immediately identify the things she needed to be fearful of. She could walk into a room without wondering if someone in that room wanted to harm her. She had full faith in the power of family. I miss those things.

I spent so many years floating in a gray haze, constantly looking for the next thing to do, the next thing to check off my list, simply trying to heal. Even before the rape, I hadn't learned the skill of living in the moment, of simply being present with whomever you are with. When it came to my kids, I was so busy constantly looking for their next step toward independence—sitting up, eating real food, potty training—that it was hard to simply focus on the moment. But in the aftermath of the rape, I had to learn how to make myself be physically and mentally present in each moment, and I have come to cherish our times as a family when we can simply be still.

I missed so many of those moments in the early years after the assault.

I still have a hard time looking back at pictures of the kids in the first few years after the rape because I don't remember most of them. Those are memories I will never get back, precious time with my husband and kids that was stolen from me.

But this hasn't just been my story. The ripple effects of sexual assault are felt far and wide. Everyone who knows me has lost something. They lost the me they knew. They lost their faith in family. They lost relationships. Their belief that bad things like sexual assault happen in other families but not ours was shattered into a million pieces, leaving nothing but slivers of what once was on the floor of their lives. This hasn't just been my story. It has been all of theirs, as well.

The woman I am today is in a lot of ways stronger than that woman who woke up on her daughter's first birthday looking forward to a day of fun, friends, and family. I've been through trauma, and I have been strong enough to heal and help others with their own trauma. I've found faith in a God who loves me and wants what is best for me. I'm surrounded by a group of friends who showed up when things were ugly and have stayed through the healing process.

And today, I'm focused on the future. Our kids are now teenagers, and Chad and I are navigating all the rewards and challenges that come with parenting teens. My business is thriving. And even though I'm nearing the end of my time in leadership on MOCSA's board, I'm looking forward to finding new ways to speak to and for sexual assault survivors.

My marriage has been to hell and back. We still think about those detectives telling Chad that most marriages end in divorce after a sexual assault. I understand why. The assault lingers in the shadows of our relationship, waiting to jump out and cause harm.

But I'm proud of us. Nearly 12 years later, we're still standing strong, and most of that is due to Chad. For years, he shouldered nearly all the responsibility for keeping our marriage together because I couldn't. I was quite literally not the same woman he married. Today, we're both different people than that young couple with small kids and a new house. But one thing hasn't changed. We're still in love with each other and looking forward to stepping into our future hand in hand.

I am not in any way grateful for what happened to me. I think if I had never been raped, my life would look different, but it wouldn't be any less fulfilling. But because I was assaulted, my life changed, and writing this book has helped me identify that some of those changes were good. Would I have rather not had to go through this particular trial to get here? Of course. But now that I am here, I can acknowledge that some good things did come out of the bad.

I think that's the reality of life, in general. We want things to be black and white, good or bad, but the truth lies somewhere in the middle. Bad things can happen, and we can get blessings out of them. They can make us stronger. They can bring us true friends. They can weed people out of our lives that don't really care about us. They can make marriages stronger. They can bring us closer to God. Those blessings don't make the bad stuff any less bad, but the bad things don't make the blessings any less good, either.

As I move forward into the next stage of my life, I take with me both the good and the bad. I venture into the future knowing that trauma is never one hundred percent healed and that healing isn't linear. I bear both the burden of my trauma and the gifts I have been given because of it.

REFERENCES

The Birthday - 2013
Jackson County Sheriff's Office. *Sheriff's Report, No. 13-07378*. Lee's Summit, MO, December 1, 2013.

The Hospital
Jackson County Sheriff's Office. *Sheriff's Report, No. 13-07378*. Lee's Summit, MO, December 1, 2013.

Jessica Bixler, et al., Plaintiffs, v. X, Defendant. No. 1516-CV22785. Circuit Court of Missouri, Jackson County, Division 15, Hon. Robert M. Schieber. Transcript of proceedings, March 27, 2017.

Telling Family
"thoughts about being able to prevent the assault": Christiansen, Dorte, Rikke Bak, and Ask Elklit. "Secondary Victims of Rape." *Violence and Victims* 27, no. 2 (2012): 246–262. https://doi.org/10.1891/0886-6708.27.2.246

Intimacy
"consented to sexual experience.": Taylor, Karen, Alyse Campbell, and Molly Hutchison. "Sexual Pleasure After Sexual Trauma." *Johns Hopkins University Student Well-Being*, April 27, 2023. https://wellbeing.jhu.edu/blog/2023/04/27/sexual-pleasure-after-sexual-trauma/.

"71% and 88% of women who have been sexually assaulted":
O'Callaghan, Erin, Veronica Shepp, Sarah E. Ullman, and Anne Kirkner. "Navigating Sex and Sexuality after Sexual Assault: A Qualitative Study of Survivors and Informal Support Providers." *Journal of Sex Research* 56, no. 8 (October 2019): 1045–57. https://doi.org/10.1080/00224499.2018.1506731.

Jessica Bixler, et al., Plaintiffs, v. X, Defendant. No. 1516-CV22785. Circuit Court of Missouri, Jackson County, Division 15, Hon. Robert M. Schieber. Transcript of proceedings, March 27, 2017.

The Importane of Therapy
"80 percent of sexual assaults are committed by someone the victim knows": The Zalkin Law Firm, LLP. "Do Sexual Assault Survivors Often Know Their Attacker?" *The Zalkin Law Firm News*, February 8, 2022. https://www.zalkin.com/news/2022/february/do-sexual-assault-survivors-often-know-their-att/.

Jessica Bixler, et al., Plaintiffs, v. X, Defendant. No. 1516-CV22785. Circuit Court of Missouri, Jackson County, Division 15, Hon. Robert M. Schieber. Transcript of proceedings, March 27, 2017.

Dissociation
Jessica Bixler, et al., Plaintiffs, v. X, Defendant. No. 1516-CV22785. Circuit Court of Missouri, Jackson County, Division 15, Hon. Robert M. Schieber. Transcript of proceedings, March 27, 2017.

"hips and pelvic region": van der Kolk, Bessel A. *The Body Keeps the Score:* Brain, Mind, and Body in the Healing of Trauma. New York: Viking, 2014.

Prosecution
"60 percent of rape victims never report the assault": National Sexual Violence Resource Center. *Statistics about Sexual Violence.* NSVRC Info & Stats for Journalists media packet. PDF. National Sexual Violence Resource Center, 2015.

"310 of every 1,000 rapes are reported to police": RAINN (Rape, Abuse & Incest National Network). "What to Expect if You Report Assault or Abuse to Law Enforcement." *RAINN – Reporting Sexual Assault to Law Enforcement,* updated July 17, 2025. https:// www.rainn.org/reporting-sexual-assault-to-law-enforcement/ what-to-expect-if-you-report-assault-or-abuse-to-law-enforcement/.

"7 percent of cases resulted in a conviction": Webster, Katharine. "Why Do So Few Rape Cases End in Arrest?" *UMass Lowell News*, April 17, 2019. University of Massachusetts Lowell. https://www.uml.edu/news/stories/2019/ sexual_assault_research.aspx.

Jessica Bixler, et al., Plaintiffs, v. X, Defendant. No. 1516-CV22785. Circuit Court of Missouri, Jackson County, Division 15, Hon. Robert M. Schieber. Transcript of proceedings, March 27, 2017.

First Anniversary - 2014
Jessica Bixler, et al., Plaintiffs, v. X, Defendant. No. 1516-CV22785. Circuit Court of Missouri, Jackson County, Division 15, Hon. Robert M. Schieber. Transcript of proceedings, March 27, 2017.

Pursuing a Civil Suit
Jessica Bixler, et al., Plaintiffs, v. X, Defendant. No. 1516-CV22785. Circuit Court of Missouri, Jackson County, Division 15, Hon. Robert M. Schieber. Transcript of proceedings, March 27, 2017.

The Trial
"rape victim dresses does create unconscious bias in juries": Beiner, T. M. "Does Target Dress Play a Part in Sexual Harassment Cases?" *Duke Journal of Gender Law & Policy*, 2007. Duke Law Scholarship Repository. https:// scholarship.law.duke.edu/cgi/viewcontent.cgi?article=1109&context=djglp

Jessica Bixler, et al., Plaintiffs, v. X, Defendant. No. 1516-CV22785. Circuit Court of Missouri, Jackson County, Division 15, Hon. Robert M. Schieber. Transcript of proceedings, March 27, 2017.

Starting a Business
The Holy Bible, English Standard Version. Wheaton, IL: Crossway Bibles, 2016.

RESOURCES

If you or someone you know has experienced sexual assault, help is available. The following organizations provide confidential support, education, and advocacy.

National Resources

RAINN (Rape, Abuse & Incest National Network)
24/7 confidential support and a nationwide service locator. Hotline – 1-800-656-HOPE (4673)
rainn.org

National Sexual Violence Resource Center (NSVRC)
Research, statistics, toolkits, and training for survivors and professionals.
nsvrc.org

National Domestic Violence Hotline
24/7 support for intimate partner violence, which often intersects with sexual violence. 1-800-799-SAFE, text START to 88788.
thehotline.org

988 Suicide & Crisis Lifeline
Call or text 988 for free, confidential emotional support any time.
988lifeline.org

VictimConnect Resource Center
Chat, text, or call for confidential referrals for victims of any crime, including sexual assault.
victimconnect.org

Love Is Respect
Support and safety planning for teens and adults experiencing dating abuse.
loveisrespect.org

DoD Safe Helpline
Confidential services for service members, veterans, and military families.
safehelpline.org

National Crime Victim Law Institute (NCVLI)
Know-your-rights resources and referrals to victim-rights attorneys.
ncvli.org

WomensLaw.org (NNEDV)
Plain-language guides on protection orders, custody, tech safety, and state laws.
womenslaw.org

State Victim Compensation Programs
Most states help cover counseling, medical costs, and lost wages. Start here and choose your state.
nacvcb.org

National Human Trafficking Hotline
Confidential help if a situation may involve trafficking. Call 1-888-373-7888 or text 233733.
humantraffickinghotline.org

SPARC — Stalking Prevention, Awareness, and Resource Center
Guides for documenting incidents, safety planning, and understanding laws.
stalkingawareness.org

Childhelp National Child Abuse Hotline
Support for children, teens, and caregivers. 1-800-4-A-CHILD.
childhelp.org

Know Your IX
Student-focused guidance on Title IX rights, reporting, and accommodations.
knowyourix.org

Treatment and Provider Locator
Search for mental health and substance use treatment that fits your needs.
findtreatment.gov

Disability Rights Network
Protection and Advocacy agencies in every state for survivors with disabilities.
ndrn.org

Regional / Local Resources

Metropolitan Organization Countering Sexual Assault (MOCSA)
Kansas City advocacy, counseling, and education for survivors and loved ones.
mocsa.org

Value Unconditional
Faith-based counseling, mentoring, and support for trauma and abuse.
valueunconditional.org

State and Local Crisis Centers
Many counties run 24/7 hotlines and advocacy centers. Check your health department website, ask your healthcare provider, or use RAINN's service locator.
rainn.org/resources

Hospitals with SANE/SAFE Programs
Call ahead to ask if a SANE nurse and an advocate are available.

Faith-Based & Community Support

Local Faith Communities
Many churches and faith communities offer confidential pastoral care,
counseling, and support groups. Ask about trauma-informed resources.

GRACE — Godly Response to Abuse in the Christian Environment
Training, referrals, and survivor-centered resources for churches.
netgrace.org

FaithTrust Institute
Interfaith tools and training for clergy and congregations responding to abuse.
faithtrustinstitute.org

For Loved Ones

Supporting a Loved One
Your steady presence matters. RAINN and local advocacy centers offer simple
guides on what to say, how to listen, and how to care for yourself.

rainn.org/articles/help-someone-you-care-about

Finding a Trauma-Informed Therapist

How to Choose
Look for training in trauma-informed care, EMDR, or somatic therapies. It is
okay to interview therapists and ask about their experience with sexual trauma.
emdria.org • traumahealing.org

Medical Care and Evidence

Forensic Exams and Follow-Up
You can seek medical care at any time. Evidence collection windows vary by state.
Ask for a SANE nurse and request an advocate to be with you.
forensicnurses.org • rainn.org/resources

Legal Rights and Reporting

Department of Justice Office on Violence Against Women
Grants, programs, and links to state and local services.
justice.gov/ovw

Note on Confidentiality
If you are under 18, mandated reporting laws may require professionals to
disclose abuse. Ask about confidentiality policies before sharing.

ACKNOWLEDGEMENTS

Before I thank anyone else, I want to acknowledge God. This book would not exist without Him. The fact that I am here, able to write these words, is proof of His presence in the middle of heartbreak and healing.

There are questions we may never have answers to. Why do bad things happen? Why is innocence lost? Why are families torn apart? God does not owe us explanations. What He gives us instead is Himself. His strength when we are weak. His people when we cannot stand alone. His promises when we cannot see the way forward.

Hebrews 12:1–2 reminds us to *"run with perseverance the race marked out for us, fixing our eyes on Jesus, the pioneer and perfecter of faith."* That is how I have endured, one step at a time. Writing this book has not been about staying in the past but about pressing forward into the future God is shaping. My hope is that in these pages you see His hand at work, redeeming even what was meant to destroy.

To Chad, my husband and anchor, there aren't enough pages to hold what you've carried. You have shouldered the weight of this trauma alongside me, without wavering. You listened when I needed to rage, sat beside me when there were no words, and believed in justice and healing even when the road was long. Your quiet strength, unfailing love, and steady presence gave me room to fall apart and the courage to keep going.

Thank you for choosing this life with me, even in its hardest chapters. And thank you, too, for the gift of vulnerability—for being willing to be raw and honest in these pages, for sharing some of your innermost thoughts and feelings when it would've been easier to stay quiet. Your words matter. Your perspective matters. And your voice adds something to this story that only you could give.

You are my greatest gift.

To my kids, you are my why. Your love has healed places in me I didn't even know were broken. My daughter, your insight and empathy go far beyond your years. You've seen more than a daughter should have to, and yet you've met it all with grace and truth. My son, your gentle spirit and quick wit brought joy back into my days when I wasn't sure I'd laugh again. I hope this book reminds you both that even in the face of unspeakable pain, beauty and love still rise. I am so proud to be your mom.

To my mom, thank you for being fiercely protective and endlessly supportive. I know this story brought up your own pain, and yet you showed up anyway, with open arms, unwavering love, and the kind of bravery only a mother knows. Your strength helped me find my own.

To my dad, thank you for your quiet steadiness and strength. You stood behind me, not trying to fix what couldn't be fixed, but making sure I never stood alone. Your presence in that hospital and courtroom and throughout this journey meant more than I can say.

To my brother Josh, you carried this trauma in your own way, and still, you showed up. Thank you for your support, your tears, and your protective heart. I know this cost you, and I see your courage. I'm grateful beyond words for the way you love our family.

To Patti, Loretta, Sarah, Jill, Anne, Dan, Nancy—and the many dear friends and family members who offered their voices to this book: thank you for allowing yourselves to be interviewed, for revisiting painful moments, and for sharing your insights with honesty and grace.

Whether your name appears here or not, please know how deeply I appreciate you. There were countless moments, gestures, and conversations that shaped this journey — far more than I could ever list. Not naming each one does not make it any less significant. Your presence, in both seen and unseen ways, has been a gift.

Through this process, I was reminded how deeply I am loved and supported. Your willingness to reflect, remember, and speak truth gave this story greater depth and tenderness than I could have written on my own. Thank you for showing up for me—then and now. There are so many of you who stood by me, cried with me, asked the hard questions, sent meals, watched my kids, or simply didn't disappear when things got uncomfortable, your presence mattered. You reminded me that even when life breaks apart, people can be the glue that holds it together.

To MOCSA (Metropolitan Organization Countering Sexual Assault), thank you for being the hands and feet of healing in Kansas City. Your advocacy, education, and compassion make it possible for survivors like me to not only survive, but to live with strength and dignity. I am endlessly grateful for the work you do and the hope you give.

To Eagle Creek Church and our community group, your prayers, presence, and love were a lifeline. You did not rush my healing or offer easy answers. Instead, you walked with me, reminded me of who I am in Christ, and helped restore my faith when I felt shattered. Thank you for living the Gospel in a way that felt like home.

To my therapist, Susan Barngrover, thank you for walking with me through some of the hardest places of my life. Your wisdom and compassion helped me untangle years of pain, shame, and silence. You reminded me of who I was before the trauma and helped me see the stronger woman I was becoming. I wish you could have read this book before you passed away. Still, I am grateful that your exact words live on in these pages and that your influence continues to guide me.

To Paul, our attorney, thank you for fighting so fiercely and tirelessly to help us receive justice. Your dedication, wisdom, and unwavering commitment carried us through some of the most challenging moments. We are deeply grateful for your advocacy, your belief in our story, and the courage you showed on our behalf. Your work made a profound difference in this journey, and I am forever thankful.

To Lori, my brilliant and compassionate writer, thank you for holding this story with such tenderness and strength. You honored every voice in these pages and protected the truth, even when it was heavy. You reminded me, over and over, that telling it was not only possible but necessary. When I didn't know how to speak, you found the words. I will never fully understand how you took what was in my heart and brought it to life on the page, but I will always be grateful that you did.

To every survivor, especially those whose stories remain unheard, this book is for you. You are not alone. I believe you. Keep going.

To you, the reader, thank you for picking up this book. Whether you come to these pages as a survivor, a support person, a skeptic, or simply someone trying to understand, your willingness to enter this story matters. I know it's not easy to read about trauma, especially when it echoes your own pain or confronts your beliefs about justice, healing, or what it means to be "okay."

If you've lived through something that tried to shatter you, I hope this book reminds you that you are not alone. That your pain is real. That your voice matters. That healing doesn't have to look perfect, and strength doesn't always look like standing tall. Sometimes it looks like breathing through one more day, telling the truth, or doing the next right thing, whatever that looks like for you.

If you love someone who has survived, I hope these pages give you insight into what it means to walk beside them, to listen deeply, and to hold space without fixing.

And if this story stirs something in you, a sense of outrage, grief, or resolve, I hope you let it move you to compassion and action. We need more people who will believe survivors, challenge broken systems, and create safe places for others to heal.

You being here is part of the story. Thank you for bearing witness. Please, keep going, with honesty, with hope, and with the kind of love that does more than survive. The kind that helps rebuild.

ABOUT THE AUTHOR

Jessi Bixler is a speaker, marketing business owner, and advocate for trauma awareness and survivor support. She brings honesty, strength, and faith to both her professional work and the deeply personal story she shares in this book. Jessi lives in Missouri with her husband, Chad, and their two children. When she's not serving nonprofits or leading her agency, you can usually find her on the front porch with a glass of wine, soaking in the quiet.

For news, resources, and future events, visit thestoryweshare. com and join the email list to follow along.

www.ingramcontent.com/pod-product-compliance
Lightning Source LLC
Chambersburg PA
CBHW021219130626
46554CB00004B/1282